# The Reign of Stephen

LANCASTER PAMPHLETS

# The Reign of Stephen

## Kingship, warfare and government in twelfth-century England

### *Keith J. Stringer*

**London and New York**

First published 1993
by Routledge
11 New Fetter Lane, London EC4P 4EE

Simultaneously published in the USA and Canada
by Routledge Inc.
29 West 35th Street, New York, NY 10001

Typeset in 10/12pt Bembo by
Ponting–Green Publishing Services, Chesham, Bucks
Printed in Great Britain by
Clays Ltd, St Ives plc

Printed on acid free paper

British Library Cataloguing in Publication Data
A catalogue record for this book is available from the British Library

Library of Congress Cataloging in Publication Data
Stringer, K.J. (Keith John)
The reign of Stephen: kingship, warfare, and government in
twelfth-century England/Keith J. Stringer.
p. cm. – (Lancaster pamphlets)
Includes bibliographical references
1. Great Britain – History – Stephen, 1135–1154.
2. Stephen, King of England, 1097?–1154.
3. Civilization, Medieval–12th century.
I. Title. II. Series.
DA198.5.S77 1993
942.02–dc20 93–18771

ISBN 0–415–01415–8

For my father and in memory of my mother,
Edward John and Muriel Addison Stringer

# Contents

vii

# Foreword

Lancaster Pamphlets offer concise and up-to-date accounts of major historical topics, primarily for the help of students preparing for Advanced Level examinations, though they should also be of value to those pursuing introductory courses in universities and other institutions of higher education. Without being all-embracing, their aims are to bring some of the central themes or problems confronting students and teachers into sharper focus than the textbook writer can hope to do; to provide the reader with some of the results of recent research which the textbook may not embody; and to stimulate thought about the whole interpretation of the topic under discussion.

# Acknowledgements

I am grateful to David King and Eric Evans for encouraging me to write this pamphlet, and for their helpful editorial comments. I am likewise very conscious of my debts to the late R.H.C. Davis, who laid new foundations for the study of Stephen's reign, and to all the authors mentioned in the 'Further reading' section. Warm thanks are also due to my students, who over the years have listened patiently to my views on the 'Anarchy' and have contributed a great deal to them. As always, however, my greatest debt is to my wife, Christine, and my children, Kirstine, Robin and Roger, for their support and understanding.

# Note on the text

To save space, references in the text have been kept to a minimum. The 'Further reading' section, while by no means exhaustive, guides readers to the most important and accessible original sources, and to those secondary works they are likely to find most helpful.

# Chronology of main events

1138–40 Stephen creates twelve new earldoms
1139     Second treaty of Durham with Scots (9 April)
         Stephen campaigns in south-west England (April–
         December)
         Stephen arrests bishops of Salisbury and Lincoln
         (24 June)
         Church council at Winchester (29 August–
         1 September) – bishops draw back from
         condemning Stephen
         Matilda lands at Arundel (30 September) and moves
         to Bristol (October)
1140     Stephen campaigns in East Anglia and south-west
         England
         Stephen's son Eustace marries Constance, sister of
         Louis VII of France
         Ranulf, earl of Chester, seizes Lincoln Castle
         (December)
1141     Stephen defeated and captured at battle of Lincoln
         (2 February)
         Scots advance to Ribble and Tees
         Angevins conquer central Normandy (April–October)
         Church council at Winchester (7–10 April) – Matilda
         becomes 'lady of the English'
         Matilda expelled from London (24 June)
         Matilda's son Henry of Anjou styled 'rightful heir to
         England and Normandy' (summer)
         Matilda routed at Winchester and Robert of
         Gloucester captured (14 September)
         Stephen released in exchange for Gloucester
         (1 November)
         Church council at Westminster (7 December) –
         bishops reconciled with Stephen
1142     Stephen besieges Oxford Castle (September–
         December)
         Matilda escapes from Oxford to Wallingford
1142–4   Angevin conquest of Normandy completed
1143     Stephen campaigns in south-west England
         Stephen arrests Geoffrey de Mandeville (September)
         De Mandeville rebels in Fenland
1144     Stephen campaigns in East Anglia, Midlands and
         south-west

Geoffrey of Anjou becomes duke of Normandy
(23 April)
De Mandeville's rebellion suppressed (September)
1145 Stephen campaigns in south-west
1146 Stephen campaigns in Bedfordshire and Berkshire
Stephen arrests Ranulf of Chester (28 August)
1147 Stephen campaigns against Ranulf of Chester and
suppresses rebellions in Kent and Sussex
Stephen's nephew William fitz Herbert, archbishop
of York, deposed by Eugenius III
Henry Murdac elected archbishop of York (July)
Robert of Gloucester dies (31 October)
1147–51 Stephen refuses to recognise Murdac as archbishop
of York
1148 Matilda returns to Normandy (February)
Theobald, archbishop of Canterbury, exiled (April–
October)
Interdict placed on England (September)
1149 Henry of Anjou accepts Scottish annexation of
northern England (May)
Stephen secures York against Scots (August)
Stephen and Eustace campaign in south-west,
Midlands and East Anglia
1150 Henry becomes duke of Normandy (January?)
Stephen campaigns in Worcestershire
1151 Eustace and Louis VII attack Normandy (early
summer)
Stephen campaigns in Worcestershire
Geoffrey of Anjou dies and Henry becomes count of
Anjou, Maine and Touraine (September)
1152 Bishops refuse to crown Eustace (April)
Henry marries Eleanor, former wife of Louis VII,
and gains Aquitaine (May)
Eustace and Louis VII renew attacks on Normandy
(July)
Stephen campaigns in Berkshire
1153 Henry invades England and takes over Midlands
(January–August)
Magnates refuse to fight at Malmesbury (January)
and Wallingford (August)
David I of Scotland dies (24 May)

Eustace dies (17 August)
William fitz Herbert reinstated as archbishop of
York (October)
Stephen and Henry agree peace terms at Winchester
(6 November)
Treaty of Westminster (December)

1154 Stephen dies at Dover (25 October)
Henry crowned (19 December)

1157 Henry recovers northern England from Scots (July)

# England, 1142–52

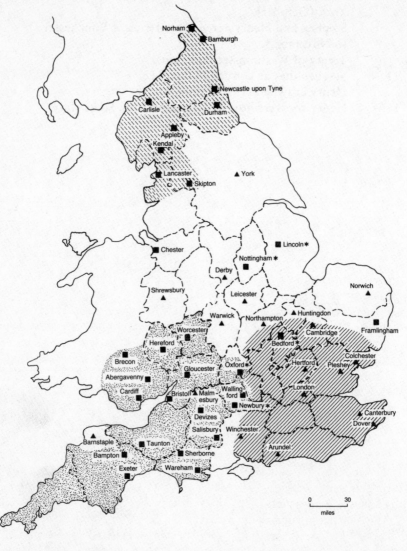

Legend:

■ Main castles held against King Stephen

▲ Other major castles

✳ Denotes castles regained by Stephen

▨ Maximum extent of area annexed by King David

▨ Maximum extent of area under Empress Matilda's control, 1142–8

▨ King Stephen's 'inner' zone

- - - - County boundaries

# 1
# The setting

## The Anglo-Norman succession of 1135

It was a vital duty of any medieval ruler to avoid instability after his death by providing for an untroubled succession. But when Henry I, king of England and duke of Normandy, died in 1135 the succession was contested, and he was succeeded not by his sole surviving legitimate child, Empress Matilda, widow of the German emperor Henry V, but by his nephew, Stephen of Blois. To many of the political elite, Matilda was unsuitable because she was a woman and married to Geoffrey, count of the Angevins, long-standing enemies of the Normans. In 1127 Henry had tried to overcome ingrained objections to the prospect of female rule by making the leading churchmen and nobles swear to accept Matilda as his heir if he died without a son by his second wife; but otherwise remarkably little had been done to help her. Her unpopular marriage to Geoffrey of Anjou in 1128 was an alliance forced on Henry by the need to prevent the Angevins from supporting his dynastic rival, William Clito, the son of Henry's eldest brother, Robert Curthose. The decisive factor, however, was Henry's reluctance to reinforce his daughter's right with enough might. Perhaps still hoping for a male heir, he refused to give Matilda and Geoffrey a power base within the Anglo-Norman state, thus denying them the strength they needed to be sure of securing the throne on his death.

Understandably provoked, they waged war on Normandy in 1135, and were still estranged from Henry and his court when he died suddenly on 1 December. Indeed, at that critical moment even Matilda's half-brother, Earl Robert of Gloucester, the old king's favourite bastard, was unable to support her succession.

By contrast Stephen, then aged about forty, was a powerful and popular figure in the Anglo-Norman world. He was the third son of Stephen, count of Blois and Chartres, and of Henry I's sister, Adela, the youngest daughter of William the Conqueror. His vast English estates were spread across twenty shires but lay chiefly in the south-east, the kingdom's political centre of gravity; he was also count of Mortain, in western Normandy, and count of Boulogne, between Normandy and Flanders. This was the kind of territorial base Matilda and Geoffrey lacked, and it gave Stephen a vital springboard to the throne. In addition, he could depend on the considerable support of his brother, Henry, bishop of Winchester, who was one of the greatest men in the English Church.

Whether Stephen acted impulsively or according to a deep-laid plan remains an open question. But with Matilda effectively out of the running he was the only contender likely to win acceptance in England, and there is no mistaking the dash and determination with which he capitalised on his strengths. First, he made for London, which immediately declared for him. Stephen was one of the city's most powerful neighbours, and as count of Boulogne he controlled its crucial trade routes with Flanders. Then he secured the royal treasury at Winchester; Bishop Roger of Salisbury, Henry I's viceroy (chief minister), put the English government at his disposal; and Bishop Henry won the all-important support of the English Church by guaranteeing Stephen's promise to uphold ecclesiastical liberties. This overcame the last remaining obstacle to Stephen's coronation: the oaths Henry I's chief subjects (including Stephen) had sworn before God to uphold Matilda's succession. It was argued that the oaths had been wrongly made under duress; some even said that on his deathbed Henry I had disinherited Matilda and nominated Stephen. That was probably untrue, but the archbishop of Canterbury, William de Corbeil, treated the oaths as void, and on 22 December 1135 crowned Stephen in Westminster Abbey.

Hitherto there had been two claims on the throne. While no

2

clear-cut rules governed the English succession, possession of royal blood was a key consideration, and another was designation by the previous king. Both Stephen and Matilda were eligible by birth; both claimed to have been designated. But in succession disputes, when one of the claimants managed to have himself formally established as king through anointment and coronation, it invariably settled the issue in his favour. Thus, whatever his opponents felt, Stephen was a properly constituted king – acknowledged as such by the pope – and this was always to be his trump card. Acceptance in England automatically carried Normandy with it, and Stephen's packed Easter court of 1136 was attended by nearly all the bishops and chief laymen from both parts of the Anglo-Norman state.

## Interpreting King Stephen's reign

After such an apparently promising start, Stephen's reign was calamitous. Although it is often supposed that he was not seriously challenged until Matilda (now supported by Robert of Gloucester) arrived in England in 1139, large-scale warfare in fact broke out immediately after Stephen's coronation. In January 1136 a general rising by the Welsh began to drive back the Anglo-Norman settlers in west and south Wales; by February the Scots had invaded northern England and secured a favourable peace; in the summer rebellions erupted in the West Country. Across the Channel, in December 1135 the Angevins had gained a major foothold in southern Normandy by seizing important castles; and in September 1136 Geoffrey of Anjou, allied with other French princes, pushed as far as Lisieux before retreating. Few reigns can have begun as perilously as this, and the situation went from bad to worse. After Matilda had launched her open bid for the throne in 1139, the critical turning-point came in 1141, when Stephen was defeated and captured at the battle of Lincoln. Before the end of that year, a royalist revival had prevented Matilda from becoming queen and secured Stephen's release. Nonetheless, the Anglo-Norman state was reduced to ruins and the king's position irreversibly destroyed. During 1141 David I of Scotland annexed northern England as far south as the rivers Ribble and Tees; Matilda tightened her grip on the West Country and the west Midlands;

and Stephen's cause was lost in France. By the autumn Geoffrey had seized central Normandy; by 1144 he had effectively conquered the whole duchy.

Although Stephen had plenty of fight left in him, he was never able to recover from these grave setbacks, even after Matilda's departure from England in 1148. Well before then, most of the important nobles had withdrawn their active support, and he also lost the confidence of the English Church, which redoubled its efforts to secure a compromise peace. Finally, in 1153 Stephen was forced to agree to the treaty of Westminster, which guaranteed him the crown but withheld it from his dynasty. Accordingly, when Stephen died in 1154 he was succeeded in England by Henry Plantagenet, the eldest son of Matilda and Geoffrey (but not, it should be noted, by Matilda herself, although she was still alive). The new king, Henry II, already had Normandy, Maine, Anjou and Touraine, as well as the vast duchy of Aquitaine; he quickly regained the northern English counties from Malcolm IV of Scotland, secured Malcolm's allegiance, and began to restore the authority enjoyed by Henry I over the Welsh princes. Thus, Stephen had presided over the disintegration of the Norman 'empire', and its fragments were gathered up within a much vaster complex, the Angevin 'empire'. One chapter in the history of medieval Europe had ended and another begun.

Why Stephen's power crumbled and what impact that had on the course of English history between 1135 and 1154 are the basic problems tackled by this pamphlet. There are two famous near-contemporary assessments. First, as Henry II's admirer, Walter Map, dismissively put it, Stephen was 'a fine knight, but in other respects almost a fool'. Second, there is the Peterborough Abbey chronicler's generalised description of the nineteen winters when 'Christ and his saints slept' and England suffered for its sins: the barons, the Peterborough chronicler said, ruthlessly exploited Stephen's weakness to assert their independence, government ceased to function, and horrifying oppressions were continuously inflicted on the Church and common people. All this was Angevin propaganda: Henry II's accession was seen as a legitimist restoration, and nothing good could be said about Stephen's regime. Nevertheless, the Angevin legend of Stephen as the archetypal incompetent king, whose realm was plunged into utter anarchy, has proved remarkably powerful even down to the present day.

4

As major recent studies of the 'Anarchy' have shown, however, the weakness of the crown affected England in complex and sometimes contradictory ways. Compared to the largely peaceful reigns of Henry I and Henry II, it was of course a period of considerable turmoil. But it is now stressed that Stephen's government did not collapse entirely, and convincing reassessments have begun to demolish the assumptions of an older generation of historians that the magnates (the earls and greater barons) were naturally inclined towards anarchical behaviour. Indeed, if attention is focused on those forces that *curbed* disorder, then it can be seen that from 1141 *three* royal governments – Stephen's from London, Matilda's from Devizes, and David I's from Carlisle – were all trying to maintain order in England. This, in turn, prompts a fresh look at how the magnates – and the higher clergy – coped with protracted warfare and the fragmentation of the realm. Did the magnates, for example, adopt independent policies primarily as a matter of necessity rather than through simple opportunism? And did they uphold effective government locally? As well as addressing such questions, we must also take account of the main ebbs and flows in the dynastic conflict, particularly Matilda's failure to dethrone Stephen in 1141 and Duke Henry's success in bringing him to terms in 1153.

Yet, inescapably, Stephen himself provides this pamphlet with its chief unifying theme. The problem of defining 'anarchy' has, after all, to be pursued firmly in the context of the failure of Norman kingship, the single most important aspect of the reign. Broadly put, the history of the Norman dominions from 1087 is the story of protracted succession crises; but only after 1135 did the strains prove too great. Why was this so?

No reinterpretation could ever place Stephen among the Titans. But it is surely unsatisfactory that, generally speaking, historians continue to explain Norman failure largely in terms of Stephen's personality, if only because they thereby conform closely to the Angevin view. R.H.C. Davis's very important and influential *King Stephen*, reissued in a third edition in 1990, provides an excellent introduction to the period as a whole; but Davis was so convinced of Stephen's personal responsibility for the disasters of the reign that at times his book reads like a study in royal incompetence. Here and elsewhere, Stephen is seen as erratic, rash, irresolute and sly: he failed to follow consistent policies, misunderstood government, and was militarily inept; he mismanaged the magnates and senior churchmen by allowing them too much power and then throwing away their support. It is assumed that his chivalrous instincts led him to make critical errors, as when he gave quarter to the garrison in Exeter Castle in 1136. Other 'mistakes' – for example, the Anglo-Scottish treaty of 1139 – are repeatedly emphasised. And no episode has earned Stephen as much harsh criticism as his arrest of Roger, bishop of Salisbury, also in 1139, for this has been thought (quite wrongly) to have destroyed the king's government and severed his relations with the Church. In sum, there is broad agreement that Stephen lacked the personal qualities necessary for successful kingship, frequently made appalling blunders, and squandered the strengths of Henry I's legacy.

A major problem for any student of the period is that such an inglorious reign invites the conclusion that all Stephen's actions were mere recipes for disaster. But what did strictly contemporary writers make of him? Their verdict was far less damning. All admired his boldness, courage, fortitude, resolve and patience. Orderic Vitalis thought that, but for the treachery of the magnates, 'he would have been a generous and benevolent protector of his country' (Chibnall 1978: 545); even William of Malmesbury, one of Matilda's partisans, believed he possessed many of the qualities required of a medieval king (Potter 1955: 20). There was thus no overwhelming feeling that Stephen was personally unfit for royal office, and this suggests that later historians have gravely underestimated him.

Nevertheless, even chroniclers loyal to Stephen had to accept that in crucial respects he failed them. The most basic duty of a medieval ruler was to defend his territories and uphold internal peace, and Stephen's poor performance inevitably provoked criticism and dismay. Some believed that a fatal weakness was the ease with which he fell under the dominance of self-interested magnates, who had too great a say in government and often gave bad advice. But even if Stephen was easily influenced, many of these men had in fact been close to Henry I, whose ability to choose responsible counsellors is not in question. In more precise terms, commentators attempted to explain Stephen's reverses by stressing his vacillation between mildness (leniency towards his enemies) and severity (abuse of church liberties). Yet such charges again miss the target, for moderation and firmness each had a proper role in royal rule, and the actions Stephen took, as Jim Bradbury (1990) has indicated, often had much in common with those of his Norman predecessors.

That brings us to perhaps the most striking point about the contemporary chroniclers. Concerned with only one part of a wider picture, they generally understated the seriousness of Stephen's predicament, a failing that modern accounts of the period have yet fully to rectify. But one contemporary observer – the anonymous author of the *Gesta Stephani* ('The Deeds of Stephen') – does provide the real key to an understanding of the reign and its problems. He concluded that no other ruler had faced such epic struggles, and by this he meant the great expansion in the scale and intensity of warfare, so that Stephen had to wage an 'Eighteen Years War' on many fronts and against many powerful enemies. As will be argued, Stephen pursued clearly defined goals in a determined and rational manner. But the seemingly endless demands of armed conflict forced him to give priority to his war effort, even at the expense of political stability; and initiatives sensible enough to start with could easily be overtaken by reverses and have unforeseen results. Those reverses, however, were largely unavoidable in the circumstances. They stemmed in essence from the difficulty of the tasks confronting him, and the most convincing explanation of Norman failure is therefore to be found not so much in the realms of Stephen's personality or policies as in pressures the like of which his Norman predecessors had never encountered. Moreover, although the fragility of Norman power did not fully reveal itself until after 1135, the causes of this fragility were *not* new; and, finally, it was Stephen's powerlessness to arrest Norman decline, more than any other reason, that alienated his subjects and made the reign so confused and troubled.

It is thus in terms of the realities of Norman power in the first half of the twelfth century that Stephen's problems must be set. More specifically, we cannot begin to explain the speed and apparent ease with which Norman dominance collapsed after 1135, and all that followed from it, without establishing the main limitations on Henry I's achievements as a state-builder. And that is the final task of this introductory chapter.

# The Anglo-Norman state and the origins of Norman failure, 1106–35

As C. Warren Hollister (1986) has shown in detail, the mastery achieved by Henry I, whom many had also regarded as a usurper king, was in many ways a remarkable one. When he became king of England in 1100, his brother, Robert Curthose, was duke of Normandy. This division of the Anglo-Norman state was totally unacceptable not only to Henry and Robert, but also to those 'super-magnates' with extensive estates in both England and Normandy, nearly all of whom supported Robert. Control of Normandy was therefore essential to Henry's security in England. Having dealt easily with Robert's half-hearted invasion of the south-east in 1101, he conquered Normandy in 1106, imprisoned Robert for life, and successfully blocked the subsequent challenges of Robert's son, the exiled William Clito, and Clito's continental allies. State power was reinforced, notably in England, where local communities came under an exceptional degree of central control. Royal justice became more widely available and feared (to his contemporaries Henry was the 'Lion of Justice'); the king's financial rights were vigorously exploited; and specialist administrators, often recruited from the lesser nobility, were unusually prominent in royal service. But although Henry's regime was exacting, he inspired a large measure of loyalty to the crown; certainly, crown–magnate relations in England, at least after the difficult early years, were far more harmonious than was once believed. Accordingly, the old view that Henry was an arbitrary monarch, whose toughness invited civil war, can no longer be taken seriously; and it has been suggested that under his strong and intelligent direction England and Normandy began to be welded into a single trans-Channel kingdom, a *regnum Norman-Anglorum*.

Henry I's reign is nevertheless one of contradictions, for while much was accomplished, his position as a cross-Channel ruler was not without serious flaws, and he failed to provide long-term solutions to the problem of maintaining Norman power. The most comprehensive thesis on the unity and stability of the Anglo-Norman state was developed by John Le Patourel (1976). But, as major articles by David Bates (1989) and Judith Green (1989b) have recently shown, Le Patourel overstated the degree

8

of internal cohesion under Henry I, and the qualifications that need to be made help to place Stephen in a more sympathetic light. One major problem left to Stephen was that there were few governmental links to foster a sense of unity between England and Normandy beneath the level of the king-duke and his household; another stemmed from the fact that Henry's power had not been spread uniformly across his lands. Most obviously, Henry had greater control in England than in Normandy, where his position was far less secure. Yet even in England some areas were less firmly under Henry's thumb than others. Above all, the north was a remote frontier zone, invaded by the Scots as recently as 1093, claimed by them as rightfully belonging to Scotland, and far from feeling the full weight of Henry's authority. Accordingly, throughout his territories Henry's power meant different things in different regions, and this also casts doubt on the notion of a compact and tightly unified Anglo-Norman state.

Again, the super-magnates formed a very influential group committed to Anglo-Norman political union; but the number of lords with *substantial* lands on both sides of the Channel has generally been exaggerated. Many magnates in reality had primarily regional interests and, since they had little to lose if the two countries were separated, their support for Anglo-Norman unity was less pronounced. In particular, lords in the frontier areas of England and Normandy often had few territorial ties with other parts of Henry's dominions, and this helps to explain why so many of them were prepared to accept Scottish or Angevin lordship after 1135. Provincial loyalties therefore undermined effective central control; in fact, as far as southern Normandy was concerned, the regional links of magnates were already causing Henry serious trouble, and William Clito received a good deal of support there, notably in 1118–19. So, for all the unifying influences at work within Henry I's Anglo-Norman state, there were significant counteracting forces, and these structural weaknesses undoubtedly contributed to its collapse within six years of Henry's death.

The durability of any state also depends on its strength relative to that of its neighbours. How secure was the Anglo-Norman state in this regard? It was Le Patourel's argument that up to 1135 'the progress of Norman conquest, domination, and colonization was a continuous and consistent process'

(1976: 27). Yet here again it is possible to take a different view: namely, that the great dynamic of Norman aggression and expansion had stagnated *before* 1135, and that the Anglo-Norman state had already begun to lose its commanding lead over rival powers.

Henry I's reign is in fact best characterised as one of imperial stabilisation, or even of imperial overstretch. Henry's policy, as has been said by Hollister, was 'not a continuation of eleventh-century Norman imperialism but a rejection of it' (1986: 249); 'the engine of conquest no longer rolled' (ibid.: 177). After 1106 Henry's basic strategy, then, was to concentrate on holding his frontiers, and that strategy was dictated largely by the problems he faced in defending Normandy against periodic assaults by the French king and the count of Anjou in support of William Clito. By contrast, Henry experienced no real trouble in England, and was able to devote the bulk of his resources to Normandy's defence. But, despite such apparent strengths, he still had his work cut out to hold his own, especially when Normandy came under concerted attack in 1118–19. Furthermore, it was a major disadvantage that the Anglo-Norman feudal levy was inadequate for permanent garrison duty or serious campaigning, and mercenaries had to be employed in large numbers (Prestwich 1981). Thus military power already depended heavily on finance, and to survive in Normandy Henry needed to exploit England's wealth to the full. But, for all Henry's achievements in English government, recent stress has been laid by W.L. Warren (1984, 1987) on administrative shortcomings and 'shifts and contrivances', with royal bureaucrats switching from one expedient to another to avoid a major collapse. The most convincing explanation of this is that even *intermittent* large-scale conflict was seriously overtaxing the system, and the strains imposed were clearly seen, at least in 1124, when the king's mutinous mercenaries in France jibbed at being paid in English coin because of its poor silver content.

All this suggests that Henry I, let alone Stephen, was not particularly well equipped to meet the demands of extended warfare. The critical factor for Henry, in fact, was the prevention of wars; but this fear of all-out conflict further compromised efforts to maintain great-power status for the Anglo-Norman state. Lacking the strength to conquer traditional enemies in France or Britain, Henry sought stability by offering peace with concessions, without necessarily resolving the original causes of tension. 'He preferred', said William of Malmesbury, 'to fight with policy rather than with the sword'; and while his alliances, notably with Anjou and Scotland, were essential to Norman security in the short term, they were gambles that in the long term simply did not pay off. Indeed, Henry himself was very conscious of the precariousness of his successes in preserving the status quo. As another well-informed contemporary wrote, 'each of his triumphs only made him worry lest he lose what he had gained'.

Thus, even before the general conflict after 1135, Norman resources already seem to have been tightly stretched, and that is another important reason for supposing that the Henrician power structure did not provide a firm basis for future success. Stephen therefore found himself succeeding to a state that was less than fully unified, and whose very survival had already placed heavy burdens on the king-duke's reserves. Nevertheless, Henry *had* dealt effectively with dynastic rivals and more or less held his ground. So, in order to complete this preliminary analysis, it is necessary to indicate precisely why Stephen should have encountered insurmountable problems in maintaining Norman power. In the last resort, Norman failure was due chiefly to two crucial interacting factors. Each provides yet further evidence of the limitations of Henry's achievement; and together they fully exposed its fragility and ultimately brought the Norman 'empire' crashing down.

The first of these factors, already hinted at, was the gradual shift by 1135 in relative power between the Norman king-duke and other rulers. For as Norman imperialism had abated, so rival powers had profited by the breathing space to strengthen themselves and generally turn the situation to their advantage – the classic fate of an empire past its prime. The English Church itself was becoming more independent of royal control under a reformed papacy which exploited Henry's difficulties to serve its own imperial ends, thus placing Stephen in a difficult position when he tried to uphold traditional crown rights after 1135 (pp. 62–3). Even in Wales, where Henry *was* expansionist, his death coincided with a resurgence under native leaders like Owain Gwynedd. But much more serious were those power shifts that saw Scotland's emergence as a new feudal kingdom in the north and Anjou's revival as a great principality in the south. Though they kept the peace with Henry I, Scottish kings were struggling to win independence from the English crown as state-builders in their own rights, and David I in particular was a major gainer from Henry's defensive strategies, with the result that by 1135 Scottish military strength was at a new high level (pp. 30–1). King David 'increased his power', wrote a contemporary admirer, 'and was exalted above his predecessors'. As for Loire-based Anjou, it had been a dominant power in eleventh-century France until eclipsed by Normandy in the 1060s. But by *c.* 1100 Anjou had begun to rise again through a remarkable programme of internal consolidation and external expansion. Former Norman-controlled Maine, an ideal base from which to probe Normandy's defences, was united to Anjou in 1110; at the battle of Alençon in 1118 the Angevins dealt another severe blow to Norman prestige by inflicting on Henry I his heaviest military defeat. Next, it was Henry's near-desperate concern to block Angevin aggression in 1128 that led him to take the momentous step of marrying Matilda to Geoffrey of Anjou. This stop-gap measure was hardly the work of a 'strong' Norman king. Rather, the Angevins had cashed in on Henry's struggles and secured a claim by marriage to the whole Norman inheritance; and that vividly demonstrated Anjou's arrival as a major power on the twelfth-century European scene.

Here, then, were two 'flank' states, both resurgent in their military might, which in 1135 had a considerable potential for expansion and were very different from the weak powers William the Conqueror had dominated. Moreover, in Anjou's case, it was in the period immediately before Stephen's reign that it enjoyed its first triumphs at Norman expense, something that makes his failure to contain Angevin pressure even less surprising.

The second chief cause of the post-1135 Norman collapse stemmed from the Anglo-Norman state's lack of a secure basis in terms of clear rules of succession – arguably its gravest weakness – and here Henry I must take his share of the blame for failing to remove uncertainties as far as circumstances allowed. As it was, the political community's rejection of Matilda in favour of Stephen finally destroyed the precarious Henrician equilibrium, and imposed staggering demands on a system ill-equipped to bear them by automatically triggering an international conflict very different in scale from earlier Norman succession quarrels. However damaging to Norman ambitions, those of 1087 and 1100 had at least been kept largely (though not entirely) within the ruling house. But from 1135 Matilda had solid support from Anjou, which was now fully committed to the conquest of the Norman dominions by every means at its disposal; the Scots, invoking Matilda's name (King David was her uncle) and their claims to the northern English counties, launched the heaviest and most sustained assault suffered by England since the Norman Conquest itself. Consequently, spasmodic Angevin-Norman and Scoto-Norman rivalries widened into a prolonged and bitter struggle, and for the first time the Anglo-Norman state was 'pincered' between two powerful and expansionist neighbours. Moreover, Angevin and Scottish enmity made it possible for civil war to persist in England when earlier it had been swiftly suppressed.

In short, when Stephen became king he faced problems that might well have broken any ruler. It does not follow that he was as able as the other Norman kings, but there was less to choose between them than has generally been thought. The main difference was that a difficult task became far harder, for Stephen was embroiled in much more than just another 'self-contained' family contest. The succession dispute was fused with a struggle for mastery between a once dominant power and rising challengers, and the military pressure was unlike anything experienced by Henry I. Thus Stephen's war of succession comprised in reality no fewer than three great conflicts: the English civil war; the Anglo-Scottish wars (1135–9); and the French wars involving 'Greater Anjou' (Anjou–Maine–Touraine) against Normandy (1135–44). He fought with remarkable stamina, resourcefulness and tenacity. Yet he faced enormous challenges, and they gradually overwhelmed him because the Anglo-Norman state simply could not cope with the new demands of general warfare. The age of assured Norman predominance in western Europe had manifestly passed, and the inevitable result was a passage of supremacy from the Normans to the Angevins and, in an obviously lesser degree, to the Scots.

# 2

# King Stephen at war

The collapse of Norman supremacy after 1135 is approached here and in chapter 3 from the viewpoints of the principal belligerents, and it is natural to begin with Stephen's waging of war. Traditional accounts tell a simplistic story of almost continuous incompetence and failure. 'Neither strategist nor tactician', runs a typical comment, '[Stephen] . . . was conventional and unimaginative, if not downright stupid' (Cronne 1970: 74). By contrast, John Beeler (1966: 157) concluded that 'in current terminology, Stephen would have been considered a good corps or divisional commander'. Though this verdict was given nearly thirty years ago, scarcely any attempt has since been made to advance the discussion, and a new assessment is long overdue.

## King Stephen's war leadership

While his deputies fought numerous separate actions, Stephen in person led great armies against the Scots (1136, 1138), the Angevins in Normandy (1137), and West Country rebels (1136, 1138, 1139–40). Although small-scale operations later became the norm, only in 1148 and 1154 was he spared strenuous active service. For manpower, he drew on feudal levies and the old English obligation to army service. But the paid troops of the royal military household formed the key element in the Anglo-Norman war machine, as J.O. Prestwich (1981) has stressed, and it was chiefly on this permanent elite force of mercenary knights and infantry that Stephen's fighting strength was based. His defeat and capture at the battle of Lincoln on 2 February 1141 cast a long shadow over the reign. Yet miscalculations were made on every side in the hostilities, and that in itself places Stephen's generalship in a less unfavourable light. More positively, his skill in setting and supporting troops in the field is reflected in a well-organised higher command system, in the use of regional military governorships and other emergency measures, and in his efforts to secure effective alliances with Scotland and in France.

But, first of all, no one has doubted that Stephen was a valiant warrior king who led from the front. Even his opponents thought him the bravest man on the field at Lincoln where, after much of his army had fled, he engaged in fierce hand-to-hand fighting until stunned by a stone. In Henry of Huntingdon's words, 'his heavy battle-axe flashed like lightning, striking down some, bearing back others. At length it was shattered by repeated blows; then he drew his well-tried sword, with which he wrought wonders until that too was broken.' He displayed the same spirited courage at the siege of Ludlow in 1139 and in the assault on Oxford in 1142. In 1147, aged about fifty, he was wounded in a skirmish.

The reign saw only two major set-piece battles, but that was not unusual in medieval warfare. Such encounters were desperately risky and best avoided, as David of Scotland also learned to his cost when defeated by a Yorkshire army at the battle of the Standard (near Northallerton) in 1138. Commanders found it hard to estimate their opponents' strength, to be sure of their troops' reliability, and to exercise overall control once action had begun. All these considerations affected the result at Lincoln, and this is another reason why it would be harsh to condemn Stephen's generalship on the strength of his performance in that battle alone.

Since Stephen made war to defend territory and his opponents to win it, castles, the decisive weapons of territorial power, played a pivotal role, and it was in the context of castle warfare that much of the fighting occurred. On balance, advances in fortress design and the sheer number of castles told against the king. England already bristled with them, far more so even than Normandy. Not every castle was strong in defence, stonework being expensive and reserved for the most important castles. But as an offensive base, a defiant castle disputed Stephen's authority by dominating its whole neighbourhood, and the mightier the castle, the more it undermined the king's peace.

Stephen fully appreciated the vital importance of controlling castles, and his grasp of siegecraft was good. He ravaged the countryside to deprive garrisons of supplies and made bold forced marches, sometimes in mid-winter, to catch them off guard. He also showed ingenuity in the means of direct assault. Different sorts of siege engines were used: 'belfries' with which to approach a castle's walls; battering-rams to shatter them; catapults to hurl missiles at or over them. Archers, slingers, miners and other specialist troops were deployed as required. Yet major castles could withstand lengthy sieges, however large the besieging armies. The technology of defence had outstripped the technology of attack and threatened to over-commit Stephen's forces by embroiling them in countless 'small wars'.

This was arguably the most important operational challenge Stephen faced, and he showed his basic tactical soundness by adopting measures best suited to these conditions. In the first place, he preferred negotiated capitulations (that is, allowing garrisons to withdraw unmolested) to pressing on with pro-tracted and expensive sieges: most notably at Exeter (1136) and Oxford (1142), after each had resisted full-scale investment and tied down large numbers of troops for three months. Another response came in the form of counter-castles, manned by only small garrisons, from which to wear down and neutralise enemy strongholds. In 1138–9 such tactics were employed by Stephen at Dunster, Ludlow and Wallingford. Finally, political action was used to seize castles that Stephen feared might oppose him. The unreliable Robert of Bampton was dealt with scrupulously in 1136 by due legal process; but, because of Robert's treachery, Bampton Castle nonetheless defied the king. Military logic urged tougher means, namely, summary arrest in the royal court of possible traitors whose release was conditional on surrender of their castles. Two powerful churchmen and two major magnates were disciplined in this way: Roger, bishop of Salisbury, and his nephew Alexander, bishop of Lincoln (1139),

Geoffrey de Mandeville, earl of Essex (1143), and Ranulf, earl of Chester (1146).

Of these tactical initiatives, the first and last have often been misinterpreted. On the one hand, Stephen's offers of safe passage to beleaguered garrisons have encouraged the view that he failed to nip rebellion in the bud – Exeter is a notorious 'mistake' – and lacked the consistent ruthlessness required for success in war. But this ignores the fact that Henry I allowed honourable surrenders at Arundel and Shrewsbury in 1102, as did David I at Norham and Wark on Tweed in Northumberland in 1138. They were a regular feature of twelfth-century warfare, much used as an efficient and economical means of taking strongpoints. And, in any event, it would certainly have been exceptional for Stephen to have refused mercy to the Exeter garrison, whose members had never sworn allegiance to him. On the other hand, the summary arrests of men at court, where they were supposed to enjoy the king's special protection, have been thought merely to confirm that Stephen displayed a unique deceitfulness and wilfully eroded support for the crown. That conclusion can be questioned on several grounds (pp. 20, 77) – including the point, overlooked by Stephen's critics, that Henry I had very probably used the same measures in Normandy. Admittedly, there was an obvious built-in limitation, for those arrested had to be released in exchange for their castles and, once released, they were free to rebel, as did Essex and Chester. But the main point here is that Stephen wanted to weaken potential opposition before it materialised and, given this, his tactics were more effective than has often been assumed. For example, the seizure of Essex's castles (the Tower of London, Pleshey and Saffron Walden) gave Stephen undisputed control of London and the south-east, and seriously hindered the earl's ability to challenge the crown. Tactically, therefore, Stephen was able to adapt to particular situations competently and with a fair amount of success.

Were Stephen's tactics related to a coherent defence strategy? His military endeavours were endless but not aimless. A successful war policy depended not on annihilating all his enemies, but on confronting them systematically and securing withdrawals from disputed areas. In pursuit of this ideal strategy, Stephen necessarily divided the burden between himself and trusted lieutenants, and there is little substance in the charges that he

17

irresponsibly ignored significant threats. In 1136 he advanced against David I and regained control of Northumberland; he saw to it that his war captains in Wales and Normandy were supplied with money and troops; and he personally suppressed West Country risings at Bampton and Exeter. In 1137 his expedition to Normandy was sufficiently effective for Geoffrey of Anjou to accept a truce. Operations in 1138, a year of mounting pressure, were scarcely conducted, as Cronne (1970: 36) put it, 'without plan or method or firmness of purpose'. In February Stephen successfully countered another Scottish invasion and harried south-eastern Scotland. But in April the Scots invaded again, and had crossed the River Tees in force by mid-August; in May Robert of Gloucester's rebellion in Normandy triggered major disturbances in the West Country and Kent. While Stephen concentrated his own efforts on the south-west, he commissioned the archbishop of York to mobilise Yorkshire's defences. Simultaneously, he sent his formidable wife, Queen Maud, to blockade the rebel garrison at Dover with the aid of the Boulogne fleet. That left him free to take a heavy toll of hostile western castles, including Hereford and Shrewsbury. Meanwhile the Yorkshire army, decisively reinforced by knights sent on Stephen's orders from the royal household, routed the Scots at the battle of the Standard on 22 August; Dover capitulated in September. In Normandy, where Gloucester's rebellion had encouraged Geoffrey of Anjou to resume the offensive in June, the Angevins were forced to retire by Stephen's field commanders. All told, this was a brilliantly coordinated defensive effort.

Nevertheless, the threats were coming from all directions, and while every major challenge had been contained, none was dealt a wholly decisive blow. The Angevins retained major Norman castles (now including Bayeux and Caen); the Scots, though defeated in Yorkshire, had not been dislodged from northern England; Bristol, the main centre of revolt in the south-west, remained defiant. The great strategic lesson of 1136–8, therefore, was that Stephen's resources were gravely overextended. To secure his frontiers and stamp out internal dissent, he had to boost his fighting strength, not least by finding ways of reducing his military commitments to a more manageable size.

These problems help to put into clearer perspective some of Stephen's most controversial measures: his 'earldom' policy of

1138–40; his peace with King David in April 1139; and, not least, his arrest of the bishops in June 1139 – allegedly Stephen's gravest blunder. As it turned out, the gains made were of limited long-term value, but the decisions taken originally had much to commend them; thus, far from acting foolishly, Stephen deserves full credit for not only identifying the constraints on his military effectiveness in 1136–8 but taking positive steps to improve it.

Stephen's 'earldom' policy, discussed more fully in due course (pp. 53–5), involved the creation of a team of especially power-ful earls or provincial governors responsible for the control of problem areas. Two earls appointed in 1138 (Worcester, York) and two appointed in 1140 (Cornwall, Wiltshire) were entrusted with particularly vulnerable regions. These men, and others like them, were now expected to shoulder more of the burden of regional defence; military responsibilities were thus thrust more firmly on to the provinces; and although this policy depended crucially on Stephen's ability to retain the earls' support, a sensible attempt had been made to relieve the pressure on royal field armies by ensuring rapid local responses to hostilities as they arose.

The Anglo-Scottish treaty of April 1139 also made good sense (pp. 32–3). The terms then granted to David I were not unduly generous and, in any case, were a small price to pay for the immediate respite they brought: namely, reduction of the triple burden of war on three major fronts so that Stephen and his war captains could concentrate on western England and Normandy. While that had been uppermost in Stephen's mind, he also hoped to enlist Scottish support for his cause, and David's son did in fact campaign with him throughout the summer of 1139; relatedly, overtures to the French king Louis VII culminated in the marriage of Stephen's son and heir, Eustace, to Louis's sister in 1140. Here, then, was a resourceful attempt to build up a powerful anti-Angevin coalition in Britain and France, and thus to win back the strategic advantage that had proved vital to Norman security before 1135.

Strategic wisdom is also seen in Stephen's vigorous assertion of the principle of 'rendability', whereby the ruler was entitled in emergencies to commandeer subjects' castles at will. In Normandy Henry I had often requisitioned castles for his war effort. As a Norman chronicler wrote, he 'used the fortresses of many of his barons as if they were his own'. Moreover, according to another well-informed commentator, Henry had not hesitated to arrest men unawares at the Norman court in order to enforce his rights (Edwards 1866: 313). But Stephen's predecessors had probably not enjoyed comparable general rights over English castles, as Richard Eales (1990) has indicated, and Stephen was determined to improve his military position by making Norman custom apply with equal rigour to England. This is the context to which the famous case of the bishops, compelled to resign their castles by their arrest at Stephen's Oxford court in June 1139, really belongs. Confusingly, historians have concentrated on the repercussions for crown–church relations and government, and have often overstated their adverse effects (pp. 50, 66–7). But, for Stephen, war needs had to come first, and the immediate strategic gains, as he correctly calculated, outweighed any costs incurred.

Admittedly, the rumours of the bishops' treasonable intentions were probably groundless; but they had nevertheless fallen under grave suspicion, and Empress Matilda's arrival in England was expected daily. Roger of Salisbury's stone castles at Salisbury, Malmesbury, Sherborne and Devizes were thought to be impregnable; and all had great strategic significance because of their proximity to Matilda's supporters in the south-west. For these reasons, Stephen was surely right to take strong measures. But, above all, what concerned him was the bishops' reluctance to cooperate fully with his war policies. As William of Malmesbury admitted, they were arrested only after they had refused to surrender their castles (or even to give temporary shelter there to royal troops), and that was an intolerable challenge to Stephen's policy, by then clearly formulated, of securing a general right of entry to English castles (Potter 1955: 27). Thus when the arrests were debated at a church council in August 1139, the king's spokesman, Hugh, archbishop of Rouen, argued that 'it is a time of suspicion [and] all the chief men, in accordance with the custom of other peoples, ought to hand over the keys of their fortifications to the disposal of the king, whose duty it is to fight for the peace of all' (ibid.: 33). Hugh's argument carried the day, and the council, though shocked by Stephen's treatment of the bishops, formally conceded his right to control at pleasure 'all fortified towns, castles and strongpoints throughout England'. Therefore, through a calculated display of royal masterfulness, Stephen had struck a major blow for the crown.

In the summer of 1139 the war thus seemed to be going well. Stephen had improved his position on all fronts in England, and Angevin attempts at expansion in Normandy continued to be blocked. His new seal, struck in July or August, has him carrying a lance with banner unfurled, as if he were poised to defeat his remaining enemies by waging all-out war against them. Matilda's appearance in England in the autumn was a bitter blow. Stephen gave her free passage to Bristol from the strong castle of Arundel in Sussex − not out of 'misplaced chivalry' (the usual argument), but to avoid a lengthy siege and to keep the opposition confined to the West Country, where in 1139–40 he was able to mount his chief effort. At that point, Stephen had victory within his grasp. But early in 1141 Robert of Gloucester made common cause with Ranulf of Chester, and the king's defeat and capture at their hands in front of Lincoln changed the entire nature of the war.

It says something for the importance of his unifying leadership that nearly all the great hammer blows to Stephen's defence strategy were inflicted during his captivity (February–November 1141), with King David's advances (despite his treaty obligations) in northern England, Matilda's consolidations in western England, and Geoffrey of Anjou's seizure of central Normandy. For the Angevins, indeed, the momentum of their conquests stabilised only when Geoffrey was invested as duke of Normandy on the fall of Rouen in April 1144. Moreover, these losses radically undermined confidence in Stephen's kingship and thus entailed major political costs that were bound further to weaken his position. In particular, many were the earls and other great lords who increasingly put their own interests before the king's and ceased to give him their full support.

The rout of Matilda's forces at Winchester in September 1141 and Stephen's liberation some two months later therefore failed to restore the status quo. The year 1141 thus saw the collapse of his 'earldom' policy, the failure of his Scottish alliance, and the contraction of his territories to little more than half their former size. Evidently, the odds were now so heavily stacked against Stephen that he had lost any hope of winning outright. Yet after his return to power he asserted a wide military dominance over Yorkshire, the east Midlands and the south-east, and he kept the Angevin party in the south-west under constant pressure. Advanced bases seized by his enemies in 1141 were retaken:

21

Nottingham (1142), Oxford (1142), Bedford (1146). He suppressed fenland revolts, put a check on the earl of Chester (1147, 1149), quashed rebellion in Kent and Sussex (1147), blocked a Scottish drive on York (1149). The most impressive instance of Stephen's operational competence in this period is provided by his campaign against Geoffrey de Mandeville in 1143–4. Supported by some 200 knights, Geoffrey occupied the Isle of Ely, converted Ramsey Abbey into a fortress, rampaged through the surrounding districts, and plundered Cambridge and St Ives. Stephen constructed a ring of castles to restrict his raiding and the rebellion collapsed when Geoffrey was mortally wounded while trying to fight his way out.

But, at the risk of over-simplifying, the general military situation in England after 1141 was in reality more or less static. Deadlock was expressed in a succession of tit-for-tat sieges and largely futile skirmishes, and in the increasing entrenchment of the main parties in their own territorial spheres. And the more warfare dragged on inconclusively, the more Stephen's political authority waned. To be sure, Empress Matilda and her supporters had limited offensive power, and Stephen dictated most of the opening moves. Nonetheless, Stephen's main western drives (1143, 1144, 1149) were turned by a combination of determined resistance and hostilities behind his front. By 1146 Matilda had lost her main forward castles save Wallingford, but by 1143 Stephen's chief bases in the south-west had all capitulated, save Barnstaple, Bath and Malmesbury. And, after 1147, the king's only concrete gain was Newbury Castle, taken in 1152 – scarcely a major breakthrough. The way was thus open for Henry of Anjou, on his invasion of England in 1153, to win the initiative and secure his hereditary rights. Yet, even then, the final outcome turned mainly on Henry's ability to exploit a political climate which, after years of stalemate, was favourable to his claims (pp. 45–8). Militarily, Stephen was never really vanquished, and it is indeed remarkable just how long his resistance lasted.

### The unwinnable war

Why then, despite his bold and resourceful leadership, was Stephen a less successful warrior king than Henry I? In essence, what he lacked was war-winning strength, and this critical deficiency was due to the interplay of three key factors. The first of these was that, quite simply, Stephen had too much to do. Henry I's successful defence of the Anglo-Norman state had rested chiefly on the restricted nature of his military tasks. To reinforce that point, since there was peace on the Scottish border, and not a single rebellion in England after 1102, Henry's main war effort was confined to France, where he could confront his enemies with a clear field behind him. Moreover, dynastic rivals were unable to pressurise him whenever they wished. Robert Curthose was Henry's prisoner from 1106; William Clito was 'a beggar in exile among foreign rogues', and could not rely on solid support from allies capable of invading Normandy in strength. Thus, only once, in 1118–19, did Henry face a genuine war of survival, as C. Warren Hollister (1986: 255) has stressed. After 1135, however, the overall strategic context was radically different. Stephen faced repeated attacks across more than one frontier by tenacious foes operating from secure bases, while sustained external hostility interacted with domestic unrest to produce a protracted civil war. So, unlike Henry I, Stephen found that his control of England and Normandy was simultaneously challenged, and he could not deal with his enemies one at a time.

Furthermore, there is the very significant fact that by 1135 the overall balance of forces had tilted against the Anglo-Norman state, with Anjou and Scotland better prepared for major conflict than had ever been the case before. Yet again, whereas through skilful diplomacy Henry I had been able to avoid the perils of encirclement and ensure lengthy periods of peace and recovery, Stephen's strategic options were much more limited. He could not repeat Henry's successes in isolating dynastic rivals from powerful allies when Anjou itself was a party to the succession struggle. He recognised the crucial importance of pacifying the Scots; but it was not in their interests to remain neutral. He concluded alliances with his brother, Theobald, count of Blois-Champagne, as well as with Louis VII; but these foundered on the complexities of French politics. The worst of it was that in 1141 Louis concentrated on intervention in Toulouse, to which his wife, Eleanor of Aquitaine, had a claim, and in 1142–4 he and Theobald were at loggerheads, thus giving Geoffrey of Anjou a free hand to roll up the opposition in Normandy. Louis recognised Geoffrey as duke of Normandy in 1144; he departed on the Second Crusade (1147–9); and when he at last decided on direct French involvement against Normandy in 1151–2, Henry of Anjou was too strongly entrenched to be dislodged.

Thus Stephen failed to secure long-term relief and often fought at a disadvantage. As a normal course, he had to disperse his forces; his opponents, by contrast, could usually concentrate theirs. Competing demands drained resources, compromised his offensive capacity and, in consequence, seriously reduced the likelihood of decisive victories. Early in the reign he fought in effect several major wars all at the same time, and his inability to concentrate on each threat in turn meant that none could be satisfactorily dealt with. After 1141, when in England castle warfare truly came into its own, rival operational requirements continued to vie with one another, and the chroniclers describe numerous attacks that were not pressed home because of the need to deal with trouble elsewhere. In 1149, for example, Stephen and his son, Eustace, found themselves campaigning in Yorkshire, Lincolnshire, Suffolk, Bedfordshire, Gloucestershire and Wiltshire – a chronic dispersion of energies and resources. As the author of the *Gesta Stephani* memorably observed,

The king hastened, always armed, always accompanied by a host, to deal with . . . tasks of many kinds which continually dragged him hither and thither all over England. It was like what we read of the fabled hydra of Hercules; when one head was cut off two or more grew in its place. That is precisely what we must feel about King Stephen's labours, because when one was finished others, more burdensome, kept on taking its place without end.

(Potter 1976: 69)

Moreover, just as the scale of the conflict was far larger than anything encountered in Henry I's reign, so were the financial costs. Though the implications have yet to be fully worked out for Stephen's wars, J.O. Prestwich first showed as long ago as 1954 how closely the military performance of the Norman kings was linked to the availability of bullion. Money provided the sinews of war: 'it is', Henry II's treasurer stressed in the 1170s, 'the abundance or want of money which raises or depresses the power of princes; those who lack it are a prey to their enemies and those who have it prey upon them.' The mercenaries of the royal household undertook the bulk of the fighting and constituted the heaviest wartime expense. Even Henry I had had to hire such troops in substantial numbers and, as has been seen (p. 10), even he had experienced difficulties in financing them on the scale required. But such problems bore far more heavily on Stephen. Not only had he to mount a much greater war effort, but for most of his reign he was significantly less wealthy than Henry had been. Thus, the second chief cause of Stephen's setbacks was that he manifestly lacked the financial means required to defend the Anglo-Norman state successfully.

Initially, royal treasure *was* abundant, and Stephen rapidly expanded his military household by recruiting warriors from Flanders and Brittany. In 1136–8 he was therefore able to launch a series of major campaigns against the Angevins, West Country rebels, the Welsh and the Scots. But the strains of maintaining war on three, even four, main fronts swiftly sapped his resources. In 1136 the siege of Exeter alone was said to have cost a staggering £10,000 – perhaps a third of his annual income from England – and such high levels of expenditure were far beyond anything Stephen could hope to sustain for long. To make matters worse, the financial base he had inherited was unsatisfactory in two fundamental respects. First, Normandy could not pay for its own war needs. Indeed, in that sense it was a distinct liability to the English crown, and only substantial injections of English silver by Henry I had averted major military reverses before 1135 (Bates 1989: 866–7). But Stephen naturally had to restrict bullion exports in order to finance his English wars; accordingly, he spent less on Normandy's defences than Henry had, and perhaps the only surprising fact is that they did not crumble any earlier than 1141. In the second place, despite Henry's attention to England's government, revenue collection was not as well organised as many historians have believed. The lack of efficient methods of direct taxation – 'the greatest failure of Norman government' in W.L. Warren's judgement (1984: 130) – meant that Stephen took over a financial system that relied primarily on exploiting royal rights of justice and feudal lordship. Such a system required constant improvisation and very careful management; it did not take much to disrupt it, and the unstable situation in England quickly undermined Stephen's ability to tap the kingdom's wealth.

Consequently, Stephen was hard pressed to sustain Henry's methods of funding military operations, and crown incomes, instead of rising to meet the spiralling costs of war, were in fact falling.

A major crisis over war finance came to a head in 1139–40. The main chroniclers all agree that by then Stephen's financial position was desperate, and that helps to explain the strategic initiatives associated with this period of the reign, geared as they were to providing a much-needed breathing space. Even so, the decision to risk battle at Lincoln may well have been forced on Stephen by awareness that he lacked the financial resources to fight a successful war of attrition. Whatever the truth of this, the long-term effects of Lincoln would certainly not have been so dire had he been able to resume military action on a grand scale. But, due to shrinking territories and increasing administrative disruption – from 1141 Stephen drew regular incomes only from south-east England (pp. 57–8) – his financial position became worse than ever. Operational effectiveness was therefore caught in the jaws of a powerful vice. On the one hand, it was hampered by immense strategic strains; on the other, it was often crippled by inadequate resources for large-scale, prolonged campaigns. In view of this, it is small wonder that so much ground was lost – and lost for good – in 1141–4.

Unpaid troops, though not in the same league as paid professionals, could still be called on. Yet here again Stephen experienced acute difficulties, and these supply the third main cause of his failures. The English feudal levy had a potential strength of about 5,000 knights, and feudal service was summoned frequently throughout the reign. But its usefulness obviously depended on the extent of the magnates' support. One basic problem was that, since few magnates in England possessed extensive Norman estates, there was a general lack of enthusiasm for continental warfare. This was not a new issue, but it nevertheless made an important contribution to Stephen's reverses in Normandy. Worse still, for reasons fully discussed later (pp. 75–9), many magnates who had previously fought for the crown refused after 1141 to support Stephen at all, or else supplied less than their due quotas of knights. In c. 1150 the earl of Leicester promised Stephen's enemy Ranulf of Chester that he would not attack him with more than twenty knights; even at Lincoln, some apparently attended Stephen with only token followings. By contrast, Henry I, with his stronger power base, had been better able to mobilise feudal forces when required. Stephen, however, had to rely more than ever on mercenaries at exactly the time when he could least afford to pay them. In consequence, his attacking power progressively declined, and he was increasingly committed to a war of limited objectives. Finally, when Duke Henry invaded in 1153, few had a vested interest in continuing Stephen's struggle, and even the royal army refused to fight. Thus, after eighteen years of unremitting effort, Stephen's war machine simply could not continue to function; and though it had done remarkably well to have kept going for so long, he had to settle for such terms as he could get.

All this suggests a more complex story than the oft-told tale of incompetent war leadership. Stephen was blighted by an excess of enemies, a chronic lack of money, and crippling shortages of manpower. He had a sound grasp of strategic-operational needs; but most of the advantages he worked hard to secure in 1138–40 were swept away at Lincoln and by irreversible financial and political constraints. As a result, during his interminable campaigning Stephen had to keep looking over his shoulder; unable to draw fully on England's resources, he also had to fight with one arm tied behind his back.

# 3

# War and the passage of supremacy

## King David I and northern England

The decline of Norman power has so far been considered in an
appropriately broad setting. In this chapter the discussion is
extended by focusing more sharply on the strengths and successes of Stephen's main opponents. The Scottish resurgence
was largely the work of one man: David I (1124–53), a formidable state-builder, whose great achievement was to lay
lasting foundations for a stronger Scottish kingdom and to
transform, albeit temporarily, the political map of Britain. Since
his English conquests did not endure, modern historians, with
the outstanding exception of Geoffrey Barrow (1985, 1989),
have tended to play down Scottish intervention in the Anglo-
Norman succession, as if David were merely championing the
cause of his niece, Empress Matilda. But although David was
sympathetic to her claims, the interests of his own kingdom
came first. His overriding goal was to advance his frontiers, and
from 1141 he effectively ruled over an enlarged Scottish realm
which, at its widest extent, included the whole of England north
of the Ribble and the Tees.

Broadly speaking, Scotland and England were natural com-
petitors in the north just as Anjou and Normandy were in the
south, for Northumberland and Cumbria (Cumberland and
Westmorland) were subject to conflicting claims by the Scottish

and English kings until as late as 1237. The Norman Conquest had put a check on the Scots, whose kingdom was in danger of being totally outclassed. When William Rufus annexed Carlisle and its region in 1092, he deprived the Scots of territories that (unlike Northumberland) had actually belonged to Scotland since the early eleventh century; and he went on to treat Duncan II (1094) and Edgar (1097–1107) as client sub-kings, partly from a natural desire to extend his influence, partly because as overlord of Scotland he could keep the border quiet. But immediately on Henry I's death, David launched a devastating offensive against northern England in a spectacular demonstration that by 1135 the regional balance of power had already shifted heavily in Scotland's favour.

It naturally favoured Scottish expansionism that other challenges constantly diverted Stephen's attention and resources away from his northern frontier; but this was scarcely the end of it. Nowhere in fact are the weaknesses of Stephen's inheritance more obvious than in his failure to control the north. It was, of course, his misfortune that, especially in times of Norman weakness, the Scots could not be expected to abandon their interest in the border shires. These, indeed, had become an even more tempting prize due to the opening up, in the 1120s, of immensely rich silver mines on the north Pennine moors at Alston and Nenthead. But there were in addition other major problems that undermined Stephen's position from the outset. The Anglo-Saxon monarchy had never been able to rule its remote Northumbrian territories as firmly as other regions; and, equally, the London/Rouen-based government of the Norman kings had only a limited hold on them. Even though Henry I created many new baronies in Northumberland and set up a bishopric at Carlisle in 1133, in reality these marchlands were, as Michael Lynch has put it, 'only half-conquered' (1992: 74). Relatedly, the Anglo-Scottish frontier, by comparison with the border areas of Wales and Normandy, was not strongly fortified, and while some castles were quite formidable they were neither numerous enough nor sufficiently well sited to halt determined Scottish attacks. That had alarmed Henry I in 1121–2, when the threat of a Scottish invasion loomed (Green 1989a: 60), but little was done to strengthen English defences. Moreover, some leaders of northern society had closer ties with Scotland than with areas farther to the south. In particular, the still influential native community in the north-west, brought under Norman rule only in 1092, had no natural loyalty to the English crown, and little sense of belonging to England at all. That helps to explain why David's seizure of Carlisle in December 1135 was unopposed, and why the men of Cumberland later fought on his side at the battle of the Standard in 1138.

But the chief of Stephen's inherited problems was undoubtedly the extent to which Scotland had been transformed by 1135 into a much stronger kingdom. At the beginning of the twelfth century, Scottish kings lacked the resources available to other European monarchs, and had limited control over their leading subjects. Nor, as has been indicated, was it clear that the kingdom could maintain its independence of the English crown. Ironically, all this would change as a result of Henry I's policies and David's skill in turning them to Scotland's advantage. Whereas Rufus had kept the Scots under pressure, Henry secured peace between the kingdoms only at the cost of concessions. Young David became a member of his inner circle, and in 1113 Henry married him to the rich heiress Maud de Senlis, in whose right David became earl of Huntingdon. But although intended by Henry to secure Norman interests, his Scottish policy (like the Angevin alliance of 1128) ultimately had exactly the opposite result. One danger was that David's marriage reinforced Scottish claims in the Borders (Maud de Senlis's father, Waltheof, had also been earl of Northumberland). More importantly, David's membership of the Anglo-Norman elite familiarised him with the strong kingship possible in a feudal state, made him determined, when he became king of Scots in 1124, to be treated as an equal to the king of England, and gave him the resources, and the opportunity as Henry's ally, to modernise his kingdom by combining the best of Scottish and Anglo-Norman practices. He reformed central and local government, introduced to southern Scotland a powerful Norman-French nobility devoted to his service, and turned the Scottish Church into a major prop of royal authority. The rising power of the monarchy ensured increased royal control over the native aristocracy, and if 'the Davidian revolution', as Geoffrey Barrow (1985: 11) has called it, still had some way to go in 1135, by adapting the strengths of the Anglo-Norman world, David was already ideally placed to profit from disunity within it. In other words, whereas David's father, Malcolm Canmore (1058–93), had merely raided English territory, the modernisation of the kingdom enabled his son to contest Norman dominance in the north as it had never been contested before.

Scottish intervention fell into two main phases: first, large-scale offensives, pressed hardest in 1138, which led to successive gains by the two treaties of Durham (1136, 1139); second, consolidation of Scottish rule over the north following its effective abandonment by Stephen in 1141. David's war machine was driven partly by his Norman followers and their retinues, who formed an elite body of some 200 knights. But in terms of sheer numbers, it was the Scottish 'common army' of bowmen and spearmen who provided the vast bulk of his fighting strength, and he could rely on native lords to bring warriors to fight in England from all the main provinces of Scotland – a clear indication of the Scottish monarchy's increased might and prestige. One contemporary observer estimated that in 1138 David mobilised 26,000 men and, though that was no doubt an exaggeration, it is abundantly clear that his mass forces (including even troops from Orkney and the Hebrides, then formally subject to Norway) were the largest hitherto committed against England by any Scottish king.

David's lightly armed native infantry were admittedly no match for an Anglo-Norman army in pitched battle, as was plainly seen at the Standard. But in skirmishing, ravaging and pillaging, these soldiers were formidably effective. Their terror tactics were on a scale not experienced since the Conqueror's notorious 'Harrying of the North' of 1069–70, and had the clear aim of so demoralising Stephen and his northern supporters that they would be forced to accept Scottish conquests, or at least a peace that went some way towards meeting David's demands. Furthermore, the Scots possessed specific strategic-operational advantages helping to tip the military balance in their favour. Scottish war treasure was scanty, but the common army fought for booty rather than pay, and so David avoided the financial costs that increasingly weakened Stephen's war effort. Having eliminated his dynastic rival, Angus of Moray, in 1130, David could also concentrate his military power in a way Stephen could not; and David was advantaged yet again because of the remoteness of northern England from Stephen's main power bases and its proximity to his own in south-east Scotland. Moreover, due to the inadequacy of English frontier defences,

David could invade almost at will. In 1136 only the mighty rock-fortress of Bamburgh proved impregnable; in 1138 the better prepared English garrisons were simply bypassed or neutralised, and the Scots swept past them on no fewer than three occasions.

Given these problems, Stephen and his deputies conducted a remarkably stout defence in 1136–8. Its effectiveness, however, depended on fielding armies strong enough to force the Scots to withdraw, or else to bring them to battle (Strickland 1990: 187–8). Early in 1136, for example, they retired (as Henry of Huntingdon reports) only when Stephen marched north with 'the greatest army levied in England in living memory'. But because of Stephen's other commitments large forces could not be spared to confront the Scots indefinitely. The heightened intensity of Anglo-Scottish warfare was thus placing an intolerable burden on his overtaxed resources, and resort to Henry I's conciliatory policies, in the hope of satisfying David and preventing further aggression, was surely the most sensible response. Nevertheless, the second treaty of Durham (9 April 1139) has been criticised by modern writers as unnecessarily generous, 'unnatural' in that it could not have lasted, and a dangerous affront to Stephen's 'natural' ally, Ranulf, earl of Chester, which should have been anticipated and avoided.

These influential opinions rest on some questionable assumptions, not least R.H.C. Davis's mistaken view that the Scots were granted the whole of northern England to the Ribble and the Tees (Davis 1990: 46). What were the treaty's actual terms? It first of all confirmed the lordship of Carlisle and the earldom of Huntingdon to David's son and heir, Henry, to whom Stephen had first given them in 1136; in addition, Stephen granted Henry the earldom of Northumberland (between the Tweed and the Tyne), while Henry and David promised they would remain 'amicable and faithful' to Stephen.

The terms offered to the Scots were not really overgenerous at all. It is true that they had been smashed at the Standard eight months earlier (22 August 1138). But this battle was fought near Northallerton in Yorkshire, 100 miles south of the Tweed; the Anglo-Norman army had failed to capitalise on its victory by marching northwards; and Stephen was too heavily engaged against rebels in the south-west to press home the advantage himself. As a result, even after the Standard, David still held much of Cumbria and Northumberland; indeed, he had regrouped his forces and was raiding County Durham. One key aspect of the treaty, therefore, is that Stephen realistically acknowledged his weakness in the north by merely confirming or granting territory the Scots already controlled. Moreover, since Henry gave homage to Stephen for Northumberland (and possibly Carlisle as well), Stephen managed to restore at least some of their conquests to the overlordship of the English crown, and in the circumstances that was something of a diplomatic triumph. Again, the Scottish undertakings to be Stephen's allies were not entirely empty promises, as Henry's actions during the following months show. He married Ada de Warenne, a half-sister of the Beaumont twins (Stephen's chief supporters), and campaigned throughout the summer of 1139 as a member of Stephen's military household. Of course, the Scots were not to be trusted if Stephen's fortunes altered for the worse, yet his discomfiture at Lincoln could scarcely have been predicted two years in advance – notwithstanding the prominent part played in it by Ranulf of Chester. Ranulf claimed Carlisle for himself, but it was not unrealistic to suppose that he would remain loyal, for he had seemed to accept its original acquisition by Henry in 1136.

Stephen's capture in 1141 presented the Scots with too good an opportunity to miss. Exploiting his difficulties to the full, they threw off their treaty obligations and dealt with the north on their own terms. Accordingly, they simply walked unopposed into north Lancashire and parts of Yorkshire, and began to draw County Durham into their orbit. David probably built in the 1140s the great stone keeps at Carlisle and Lancaster and the 'new castle' of Tulketh near Preston. Thus the Scottish occupation obviously had a military basis; but from 1141 David controlled the north less as a conqueror and more as a lawful and responsible ruler who provided an acceptable alternative to Stephen. All the main northern English chroniclers now had nothing but praise for David, and felt that the beneficial effects of his government more than compensated for the earlier Scottish atrocities. John of Hexham thought that no contemporary king had greater virtues, and stressed David's vision and courage in tempering 'the fierceness of his barbarous nation'. Ailred of Rievaulx, who knew David especially well, emphasised his wisdom and compassion, his love of justice, and his devotion to the Church. William of Newburgh, a late but reliable source, believed that it was under David that royal government was most effective in England during the 1140s and early 1150s. As he put it, 'the north country, which as far as the River Tees had fallen under the power of David, king of Scots, was peaceful, thanks to his diligence' (Walsh and Kennedy 1988: 99).

Many indeed were the ways in which David stressed the acceptable face of Scottish power and thereby consolidated his position in the north. He swiftly made grants of privileges to woo the northern Church, whose support was vital to effective control. Charters of protection were issued for all the main monasteries and their possessions (anyone who threatened them would have to answer to David or Earl Henry). New gifts were made to the priories of Brinkburn, Hexham, Tynemouth and Wetheral; even St Bartholomew's Priory at Newcastle upon Tyne, a small Benedictine nunnery, gained fresh endowments. Athelwold, bishop of Carlisle, quickly accommodated himself to the changed order, but a complex situation unfolded at Durham, where events did not all go David's way. Durham, far more than Carlisle, was a formidably powerful bishopric, and David naturally tried to force through the election of one of his own men, his chancellor William Cumin, to the vacant see in 1141. But the Durham monks preferred another candidate, and bitterly resented the arrogance of Cumin, who occupied Durham Castle, acted as a pseudo-bishop, and harshly oppressed them. They put themselves in the hands of the pope, Bishop Henry of Winchester (the papal legate), and Stephen, with the result that William de Sainte-Barbe was consecrated bishop in 1143. David prudently disowned Cumin and helped Bishop William to gain full possession of the see in 1144. Even so, despite David's skill in distancing himself from Cumin's high-handed behaviour, Durham was always wary of Scottish overlordship, and in 1153 the chapter elected as their next bishop Hugh du Puiset, who was none other than Stephen's nephew.

The case of Durham shows that the transition from Norman to Scottish rule was not always smoothly achieved; but in general David consolidated his power speedily and thoroughly. His relations with the nobility bear out that point. Major changes took place in the Scottish interest to complement Henry's position as earl of Northumberland. Thus David's nephew, William, son of King Duncan II, gained both Allerdale (north-west Cumberland) and Copeland (south-west Cumberland), and by 1151 controlled the Yorkshire honour of Skipton and Craven. Hugh de Morville, Constable of Scotland, took over the lordship of Appleby (north Westmorland) and probably had authority over Kentdale (south Westmorland). The dominance enjoyed by these potentates, and by Earl Henry, clearly brought the north more firmly into David's hands; but, significantly, this was achieved with the minimum possible disruption to existing landowners. In effect, an extra tier of lordship was superimposed without the necessity of dispossessing established nobles, and that enabled David to give his regime strength in depth by cultivating their support. Accordingly, they were offered in return for their loyalty security for their lands and the possibility of some advancement; and most did submit to Scottish overlordship. Some were reluctant about it, yet submission was made easier not only by David's moderate policies and the protection he offered, but by the fact that few had major estates in areas firmly under Stephen's control in the south (Green 1990: 93). In that respect, feudal geography played directly into David's hands, for failure to support him would normally have led to the loss of a family's most valuable lands.

From 1141 David thus reinforced his influence through a mixture of firmness and conciliation. But any analysis of his achievements must also stress that the northern counties (at any rate Cumberland, Westmorland and Northumberland) were thereby firmly absorbed into the Scottish kingdom. With Earl Henry as his right-hand man, David ruled them in complete independence of Stephen – a marked contrast to the position agreed in 1139 – and acknowledged no other superior. That was made very plain when in 1149 the sixteen-year-old Henry of Anjou, having supplanted Empress Matilda as claimant to the English throne, arrived at David's court in Carlisle. He was then in no position to insist on any rights of overlordship such as those formerly reserved by Stephen; in fact, he specifically promised (according to William of Newburgh) that if he became king of England he would leave the Scots in possession of the north, and thus seemed to accept that it no longer formed part of the English realm (Walsh and Kennedy 1988: 101). Such a conclusion is also supported by the fact that when, on the same occasion, Ranulf of Chester surrendered his claims to Carlisle in return for north Lancashire, he gave homage for the latter not to Henry of Anjou, but to David himself.

Moreover, the powers David and Earl Henry exercised in northern England were no less royal than those they held in Scotland, where Henry – as king-designate – also ruled in association with his father. They supervised the sheriffs and justices, controlled the royal castles and royal forests (notably Inglewood Forest), appropriated royal revenues, and took over the royal mints at Carlisle, Corbridge and Bamburgh, where they issued coins in their own names. In these ways they claimed and achieved sovereign power, replacing Stephen's with their own. They constantly travelled back and forth with their households, regularly held court at Carlisle and Newcastle, and gave more personal attention to the region's affairs than any king of England had ever done before. Unification was eased by the fact that 'Normanised' southern Scotland and northern England were at equivalent stages of development, by the issue in c. 1150 of a common royal coinage for the two areas, and by the emergence of an influential group of Anglo-Scottish landholders strongly committed to continued political union. One such was Hugh de Morville, lord not only of Appleby but of Cunningham in Ayrshire and of Lauderdale in Berwickshire. It was, indeed, as if the north was bound more tightly to Scotland than it had ever been bound to England.

Nor is there any reason to conclude that David was satisfied in the 1140s with expanded dominions that included Cumbria and Northumberland (and even north Lancashire and County Durham). It was in 1149 that he formed an alliance with Henry of Anjou and Ranulf of Chester for an advance on York. He was also supported by Henry Murdac, archbishop of York, whom Stephen regarded as an enemy and had kept from his see since 1147 (pp. 65–6). Possibly David was placing Angevin interests before his own, but there is an alternative and more attractive interpretation. A Scottish takeover of York would have immeasurably enhanced David's influence, and for one very important reason. If the new 'Scoto-Northumbrian' kingdom were to be fully formed, control of York was the logical next step, for not only did the archbishopric have jurisdiction over its suffragan bishoprics at Durham and Carlisle, but it also threatened David's position by claiming authority over the Scottish Church itself, which had no archbishopric of its own. In 1149, however, Murdac was not in the homage of the English crown. David therefore had the opportunity of installing him in York as his own archbishop; and a new kingdom with its twin capitals at Edinburgh and York would have cocooned the Scottish Church (together with Durham and Carlisle) within a politically unified and fully independent church province. But it was Stephen who pre-empted David by arriving at York in sufficient strength to force him to back down. Stephen went on to reach an accommodation with Murdac in 1151, and it was probably no coincidence that in the same year David revived with the papacy the question of creating an archbishopric at St Andrews. Even at the height of their power, the Scots thus faced in Stephen a worthy adversary whose grip on his remaining northern territories could not be shaken.

But little yet suggested that, farther to the north, the Scoto-Northumbrian kingdom would not go from strength to strength. A significant event occurred in 1150 when Earl Henry founded a Cistercian abbey at Holm Cultram in Cumberland. His foundation charter conveys no sense that Cumberland stood apart from the Scottish realm. Quite the reverse in fact, for Henry stipulated that the monks were to enjoy as much peace and liberty as Melrose Abbey enjoyed through the favour of his father. Melrose, the senior Cistercian abbey in Scotland, was the mother-house from which Holm Cultram's founding community of monks was drawn, and their very arrival in Cumberland showed how irrelevant the former Tweed–Solway frontier had become. But the balance of forces was nonetheless about to swing back in England's favour, due partly to Henry II's uncontested succession in 1154 and partly to unrelated Scottish misfortunes. Earl Henry's premature death in 1152 meant that when David himself died at Carlisle in 1153, he was succeeded not by a mature and experienced heir, but by his grandson Malcolm IV, a boy of only twelve. That was an obvious disaster for the Scots, the more so because Malcolm faced attacks from the Hebrides and Highland risings. Henry II therefore held all the cards, and in 1157, contrary to his promise in 1149, he compelled the Scots to surrender the northern shires on the grounds that he 'ought not to be defrauded of so great a part of his kingdom'.

## Empress Matilda, Duke Henry and the English succession

Angevin war aims were fundamentally different to Scottish ones. The overriding objective was the complete takeover of

37

Norman power, and this section focuses on the main stages by which that was achieved. Thanks to the invaluable work of Marjorie Chibnall, Empress Matilda's recent biographer, there is now no risk of understating the importance of Matilda's contribution to this process (Chibnall 1988, 1991). Earlier writers concentrated on her humiliating failure to topple Stephen in 1141, stressed the personal shortcomings that the pressures of that extraordinary year brought to the surface, and virtually ignored other aspects of her career. Admittedly, so discredited was Matilda by her expulsion from London in 1141 that she retained support only by immediately transferring her hereditary claims to Henry, her eldest son, as 'the rightful heir to England and Normandy'. But before and after 1141 she nevertheless acted constructively to advance Angevin might. She intervened in England at a crucial moment and successfully revived a flagging cause, established a major English stronghold for the Angevins, and, after she had renounced her rights in favour of Henry (who in 1141 was only eight years old), worked vigorously for his succession. These issues will be dealt with first; then follows an analysis of the reasons for the contrasting fortunes of Matilda and Henry in 1141 and 1153 respectively.

On the eve of Matilda's landing in England on 30 September 1139, Stephen held a clear military advantage (pp. 18–21). Moreover, Pope Innocent II had recently refused to reverse his recognition of Stephen on Matilda's appeal that she had a better right to the crown. It was, in the circumstances, a brave decision by Matilda to challenge Stephen head on, and her arrival turned internal unrest into full-scale civil war. Matilda's following among the magnates was small, but three great lords put their weight behind her: Earl Robert of Gloucester, her half-brother and commander-in-chief, Miles of Gloucester, and Brian fitz Count. These men were especially strong in the West Country and the Marches of south Wales, and all were veteran military captains. They gradually turned the south-west into an Angevin power base, with its bastions at Bristol, Gloucester and Devizes protected by Brian fitz Count's forward outpost at Wallingford in the Thames valley. The prestige of controlling part of the kingdom gave Matilda the opportunity to capitalise on Stephen's political troubles by acting as a natural rallying-point for opposition to the crown. And on 2 February 1141, in alliance with the disaffected Ranulf of Chester (Gloucester's son-in-law),

Matilda's forces secured at Lincoln a potentially war-winning victory.

The rout of Matilda's army at Winchester seven months later failed to cancel out the effects of Lincoln, for the recovery of Stephen's position in England was only partial and unaccompanied by any comparable revival of his fortunes in France. Indeed, in Normandy the Angevin steamroller advanced remorselessly: in 1141 Geoffrey of Anjou conquered its central core; in 1142–3 he seized much of western Normandy; in April 1144, when Rouen Castle fell, he assumed the title of duke. Thereafter Duke Geoffrey's government of the duchy was more effective than Stephen's ever had been, so comprehensive was this expansion of Angevin supremacy. In England itself, Matilda's forces never recaptured the military initiative, and were often on the defensive – sometimes desperately so, as in December 1142 when, camouflaged against the snow in a white cloak, Matilda had to make a daring night-time escape through enemy lines from Oxford to Wallingford. But Stephen was unable to prevent them from entrenching themselves in a broad area extending from Herefordshire to Berkshire, and from Wiltshire to Cornwall. Furthermore, Matilda and her supporters were just as concerned as the Scots to establish a powerful 'state' in the territories under their military control. Matilda's brief moment of triumph in 1141 had brought her enhanced authority as 'lady of the English' (p. 41), and she now strove to strengthen her regional dominance by acting as a legitimate ruler in her son's name and replacing Stephen's government with an administration of her own, based first at Gloucester, then at Devizes. As a local chronicler put it, she 'exercised the prerogatives of the English crown at her pleasure'.

Matilda's party had considerable knowledge of royal bureaucracy and its procedures. Earl Robert was in effect resuming the role of chief royal counsellor that he had held under Henry I, while Matilda's household – the hub of her administration – not only was modelled on Stephen's, but contained stewards, chamberlains and constables (including Brian fitz Count and Miles of Gloucester) who had previously served the crown. Miles was also a highly experienced sheriff and royal justice. All this helped Matilda to strengthen her region through the exercise of royal authority, and other essential aspects of a regular royal administration appeared. Coins were minted in her name at Bristol, Cardiff, Oxford and Wareham; she dispensed justice, as when she restored the land of Longleat to Cirencester Abbey; her scribes issued charters in regal form, as when she granted the royal manor of Blewbury to Reading Abbey in recognition of 'the devotion and loyal service of Brian fitz Count'. Her charters also assumed the existence of a well-organised financial and judicial system in the shires, based on sheriffs, justices and other officials. But just as in the late 1130s earls became the linchpins of Stephen's government in the localities (pp. 53–5), so Matilda relied heavily on Earl Robert and the new earls she herself created, the majority in 1141, for Cornwall, Devon, Hereford (Miles of Gloucester), Oxford, Somerset with Dorset, and Wiltshire. Their task was to oust Stephen's earls and annex counties as complete administrative units by making themselves responsible for local defence and good order. Some often put their private interests first, but strong hands were nonetheless at work. Indeed, according to the *Gesta Stephani*, in the early 1140s Earl Robert and his supporters put the whole area from the Bristol Channel to the south coast 'under their own laws and ordinances ... restoring peace and quietness everywhere' (Potter 1976: 151). Admittedly, military disruption (especially in the counties closest to Stephen's) and problems of disloyalty meant that the south-west never enjoyed the sustained stability that northern England did under King David, or Normandy under Duke Geoffrey. But the main point is that through administrative consolidation Matilda's hegemony was given a greater solidity, and thereby her region was brought more firmly under Angevin dominance than would otherwise have been the case.

So political control was strengthened, and the West Country and west Midlands became a fairly powerful provincial 'kingdom' ruled by Matilda as regent for the young Henry. In fact, it was strong enough to survive even Gloucester's death in 1147 and Matilda's departure for Normandy in 1148. Militarily and politically, therefore, Matilda had a vital part in ensuring that in the 1140s Henry's youth was merely a theoretical advantage for Stephen. She prepared for Henry's succession by giving him time to establish himself as a leader capable of acting for himself, by creating an indispensable English base from which to press his claims, and then, after her return to Normandy, by advising and supporting him as a member of his inner circle. In sum, Marjorie

Chibnall concludes, Matilda played the 'roles of regent, adviser, and transmitter of the English crown with more success than has sometimes been recognised' (1988: 129).

The two most basic questions can be taken together. Why did Matilda fail to win in 1141? Why was Henry successful in 1153? Briefly stated, in 1141 Matilda was unable to convince a sufficiently large section of the political community in England that they would fare better under her leadership than they had done under Stephen's, whereas in 1153 Henry could make men believe that he would protect their interests, restore harmony, and be a worthy monarch. But their differing fortunes are not to be explained solely on the grounds that Matilda threw away support while Henry was more adept at attracting it. As will be seen, Matilda's high-handed and insensitive behaviour in 1141 undeniably fell far short of contemporary expectations. Even so, it must be recognised that she pursued a more demanding strategy than her son would do twelve years later, and embarked on it lacking certain important advantages Henry enjoyed, not the least of which was the ability to learn from her mistakes.

By the peace terms agreed at Winchester on 6 November 1153, and confirmed in December by the treaty of Westminster, Henry recognised Stephen as king of England for the rest of his life, and Stephen adopted Henry as his heir to the kingdom. Such a compromise did not question Stephen's right to the throne, embarrass the Church, and invite renewed strife. In 1141, however, Matilda wanted unconditional victory. She was thus committed to supplanting Stephen and, despite his capture at Lincoln, that automatically lengthened the odds against her.

Nine weeks after Lincoln, at a church council convened at Winchester (7–10 April) by Stephen's brother, Henry, bishop of Winchester and papal legate, Matilda was recognised as *domina* ('lady' or 'ruler'). This acknowledged her right to wield royal power, but she was still a vital step from the throne. A formal crown-wearing might just have satisfied her, for she had already been anointed queen ('empress' was a courtesy title) as consort of the king-emperor Henry V of Germany, her first husband. It is far more likely, however, that she wanted to establish her constitutional status unequivocally with a full coronation according to English ritual. Either way, of course, she never became queen of England.

Most modern accounts assume that in April 1141 the English

41

Church's support for Matilda's crowning was secure, and that she would have swiftly been accommodated but for the unavailability of Westminster Abbey due to opposition from the Londoners, who were among Stephen's staunchest adherents. This interpretation presents considerable difficulties. After all, although Westminster was the recognised venue for English coronations, in emergencies a compliant Church would conduct them elsewhere, as when Henry III was crowned at Gloucester in 1216 because London was occupied by the French. In reality, Matilda had to accept that few bishops were deeply committed to her cause. Even Henry of Winchester, whose temporary desertion of Stephen has been much criticised, deserves some sympathy when he later protested that he had accepted her as lady only under duress. Moreover, although a captive and unable to fulfil his royal duties, Stephen retained God-given authority as the anointed and lawful monarch – as the *Gesta Stephani* stresses, 'though he was kept among his bitterest enemies they still could not prevent his being king' (Potter 1976: 113) – and it seems most improbable that Archbishop Theobald of Canterbury, whose right it was to carry out the coronation, would have crowned Matilda unless Stephen had stood down.

In fact, respect for Stephen's royalty was such that Theobald and most bishops were reluctant to slight the king in any way. Proof of this comes from their refusal to swear fealty to Matilda as lady until they had obtained Stephen's permission to adapt 'as the times required'. Even Matilda's becoming *domina*, let alone queen, had presented problems. Many senior churchmen were therefore uneasy at having to take sides against the lawful sovereign, and no doubt regarded Matilda's rejection of dynastic compromise as a serious blow to the prospects for political stability. In these circumstances, they could not give her their full backing, and it is an indication of Bishop Henry's fears for the welfare of the Church and realm that he agreed to support her only for as long as she upheld ecclesiastical rights and consulted him on public business. A coronation for Matilda thus appears to have turned on her ability to make Stephen's position completely untenable. The horrific crime of regicide, if ever contemplated, was too extreme a solution. Robert of Gloucester, wrote William of Malmesbury, 'had regard, even in the person of a captive, to the splendour of the crown' (Potter 1955: 49). Deposition required papal agreement and pressure, but Innocent

II remained on Stephen's side; nor was the king likely to abdicate unless Matilda established such an unchallenged personal supremacy that he had no alternative but to concede.

But the attitude of the magnates was also an acute problem for Matilda. After Stephen's capture, many ceased to support him actively, but they did not renounce their allegiance to the crown, and were by no means convinced that their best interests would be served by accepting her leadership. In addition, the Londoners' refusal to admit Matilda to the city until June allowed Stephen's queen, Maud of Boulogne, to retain control of the south-east, marshal the king's forces, and drive home that Matilda was far from holding sway throughout the country. So, although Geoffrey of Anjou was making rather better progress in Normandy, Matilda badly needed committed allies early in 1141. Her court remained small, and many powerful figures were simply waiting to see what would happen. Accordingly, the importance of London–Westminster, at the heart of Stephen's power base, was more political than ceremonial, for her hopes of becoming queen depended on taking over the royal capital and then exploiting the situation properly in order to attract broad-based support.

When Matilda at last entered London in June (she was driven out a week after its grudging submission), 'it was thought', reported William of Malmesbury, 'that she might at once gain possession of the whole of England'(Potter 1955: 56). London's fall should indeed have been decisive. The city was 'the queen of the whole kingdom', and its seizure at first persuaded the king's party that further resistance was pointless. But Matilda's brief occupation of London is a notorious period of self-inflicted disaster. In fairness, the demands imposed on her continued to be severe: she did not have much scope for error in a man's world, and powerful competing interests had to be satisfied. Yet Matilda did very little to help herself and merely reinforced prejudices against female rule.

At London, Bishop Henry (and Robert of Gloucester) tried to persuade her to set the kingdom's affairs in order. But it was later said on Henry's behalf that she disregarded his advice, wilfully alienated the magnates, and broke her promise to respect the freedom of the Church. That she intended to reintroduce lay investiture (p. 62) is now discounted, but her meddling in ecclesiastical matters was sufficiently indiscreet to cast suspicion on her attitude towards church liberties. Most damaging of all, however, was her desire for revenge. Her vindictiveness was well seen when leading notables arrived in London and promised to prevail on Stephen to abdicate in her favour, provided he were set free; clearly intent on imprisoning Stephen for life, she recklessly provoked them by rejecting their proposals out of hand. She also turned down Queen Maud's request, endorsed by Bishop Henry, for fair treatment of Stephen's elder son and heir, Eustace, by granting him his father's counties of Boulogne and Mortain. This stung the queen into renewing the war and helped her to rally support, for such intransigence offended the magnates' deepest instincts. Above all, the great lords wanted assurances about their inheritances, the bedrock of their wealth and prestige; but to disinherit Eustace of lands Stephen had lawfully gained from Henry I was a blatant infringement of property rights, and caused widespread alarm that Matilda might confiscate their most prized possessions. Indeed, it was already known that she had arbitrarily seized the estates of certain nobles, despite their offers of submission, and was unwilling to confirm grants made by Stephen, a policy bound to antagonise all who had profited from his patronage. To make matters even worse, she demanded unreasonably heavy taxes from London itself, and churlishly refused to renew the city's old laws.

In short, what cost Matilda the throne in her hour of apparent victory was her failure to secure the all-important middle ground by acting with mercy and moderation in general and by upholding subjects' rights and liberties in particular. Queen Maud ably exploited the mounting sense of outrage and resentment, and gave Matilda a sharp lesson in leadership. The support of the Londoners and Bishop Henry was quickly regained; others Maud wooed 'by prayer or price'. Geoffrey de Mandeville, who had helped Matilda to enter London, deserted her, and even Ranulf of Chester tried (albeit unsuccessfully) to rejoin the king's camp. Reduced largely to the 'old guard' of the Angevin party, Matilda's forces were dispersed by the queen's army (including the London militia) at Winchester on 14 September. Robert of Gloucester was captured while covering Matilda's disorderly retreat to the West Country, and he was exchanged for Stephen in November. The English Church publicly renewed its allegiance at Westminster on 7 December, and Stephen spent Christmas at Canterbury where he solemnly wore his crown to symbolise his return to power.

By 1153 the context of the dynastic struggle had changed a great deal, and in some respects, though not in others, Henry was very strongly placed. His masculinity gave him an obvious advantage over his mother. Furthermore, the few major fluctuations of military fortune after 1141 had favoured the Angevins rather than Stephen. As he bitterly protested to the pope in 1148, he had been despoiled of parts of England and the whole of Normandy. By contrast, Henry, though still young, established between 1150 and 1152 a phenomenal ascendancy by amassing lands that swept from the Channel to the Pyrenees and gave him control of half of modern France. In 1150 Geoffrey of Anjou put him in charge of Normandy, a master-stroke designed to strengthen Henry's hand in winning the support of the super-magnates, whose interests lay as much in Normandy as in England. Then, on Geoffrey's death in September 1151, Henry inherited Anjou, Maine and Touraine; in May 1152, his marriage to Eleanor, the divorced wife of Louis VII, brought into his hands the duchy of Aquitaine, the largest of all the French principalities. Henry had the added advantage of an English power base, and so in 1153 Stephen found himself confronted by an enemy who had considerably more land and wealth than he did himself, and thus greater military reserves and more scope to attract support.

By 1153 Stephen had also to accept that most magnates, while reluctant to switch their allegiances to the Angevins, were disillusioned by his inability to provide the security and advancement they needed and expected, and had long since withdrawn from his court to protect their own interests. Some, of course, exploited the situation for their own ends; but the majority desired a return to peace and stability. Similarly, the English bishops, whose overriding concern was the harm protracted warfare was inflicting on the Church, had everything to lose from a continuation of hostilities. The underlying loyalty of both groups was to the crown; but they wanted some kind of reconciliation between Stephen and Henry, and were totally opposed to the king's war aims, which now focused on securing the throne for his heir, Eustace.

How far the political pendulum had swung against Stephen can, indeed, best be seen from his efforts in 1152 to have Eustace crowned as his co-ruler and successor. In France it was the normal practice of the Capetian kings to ensure the succession by crowning the heir in his father's lifetime. But there was only one very distant precedent for this in England, and Stephen's stratagem must be regarded as a desperate innovation designed to secure his dynasty by presenting Henry with a *fait accompli*. Yet at London in April 1152 the English bishops, with papal backing, unanimously refused to crown Eustace. In other words, they rejected Eustace's claims on the throne and implicitly recognised the strength of Henry's hereditary title. Stephen had no choice but to try to regain the initiative through a military challenge; but Henry's successful defence of Normandy in the summer of 1152 against the combined forces of Eustace *and* Louis VII (Eustace's brother-in-law) merely confirmed his emergence as a leader of European stature, well able – unlike Stephen – to defend his territories and protect his subjects.

For all these reasons the ground had already been well prepared for the final Angevin victory. Yet this does not mean that on Henry's invasion in January 1153 his *active* support in England was extensive. In fact 1153–4 was a critical transitional period, for, as Graeme White (1990) has recently stressed, Henry's ultimate succession was not as cut and dried as has often been assumed. First, in 1153 Stephen remained firmly planted in London and the south-east; thus, hard pressed though he was – Henry had virtually full control of the Midlands by July or August – Stephen's personal position was obviously much stronger than it had been during his captivity in 1141. Second, the need to maintain his continental defences meant that Henry was at far less than his full strength: in consequence, while it is true that the royalist army refused to fight against Henry's forces at Malmesbury and Wallingford, his followers were as loath as Stephen's to risk a military showdown. In any case, it was widely recognised, especially after Lincoln, that battles might achieve nothing save baronial forfeitures and further misery for the Church. In the third place, and perhaps most critically, Stephen could still rely on a deep-seated reluctance to engage in rebellion. That was partly because all but the extremists on either side were set on peace. But as in 1141, so in 1153, a key issue was the political community's fundamental respect for the prestige of the crown. Thus, however sympathetic to a change of *dynasty*, the bishops and moderate magnates would not back Henry's succession if that meant overthrowing the reigning monarch. So while few would fight for Stephen, many would not fight against him, and even among the super-magnates, in any event few in number, Henry probably could not rely on unconditional support, however much their Norman lands drew them to his side.

Henry's future depended on his ability to 'read' these basic facts of Anglo-Norman politics. Unquestionably, he ideally did not want a compromise peace, but he did not allow his frustration to cloud his political judgement. Indeed, it was Henry's good sense in lowering his expectations and avoiding any repetition of his mother's mistakes that provides the real reason why he was successful where Matilda had failed. It was probably at Wallingford, early in August 1153, that Henry finally accepted that an outright triumph was beyond his grasp; the basic question, therefore, was how to bring Stephen to terms. Compromise over the crown was crucial – without it there would have been no Angevin success at all. But also important was the fact that *throughout* 1153 Henry made concessions and thereby built up overwhelming support, if not for Stephen's dethronement, then at least for his own succession. He dealt fairly with individual magnates, including old enemies, and reassured them about their family properties. According to the *Gesta Stephani*, 'some he admitted to his favour by amicable agreement, others he won over by promises and liberality, all he met affably and graciously as occasion and necessity required' (Potter 1976: 235). Thus the earl of Chester and the earl of Leicester (the latter once one of Stephen's closest allies) obtained confirmations of their inheritances and major new endowments besides. In such ways Henry put increased pressure on Stephen, the more so because the king lacked the power to match such displays of 'good lordship'. Admittedly, luck made a vital intervention on the Angevin side in the form of Eustace's premature death from a sudden illness in August 1153. Eustace, Henry's sworn enemy, would never have given up fighting for the crown, and his departure so demoralised Stephen that, according to William of Newburgh, he 'listened more patiently than usual to those urging peace' (Walsh and Kennedy 1988: 127). But Henry also showed his political wisdom when he bought off the claim to the throne of Stephen's younger son, William, by immediately confirming to him his gains as earl of Surrey and all his father's private lands, including Boulogne and Mortain. In addition, William was offered Norwich and the whole county of Norfolk

– a very generous settlement which, all told, made him the most powerful magnate of all.

The higher clergy, too, were treated very differently by Henry and Matilda. Henry developed close ties with Archbishop Theobald of Canterbury, the chief go-between in the lengthy peace negotiations, and repeatedly stressed his concern for clerical interests. For example, he prohibited looting by his troops and banished those guilty of pillaging Malmesbury Abbey; he swore to restore to the bishopric of Salisbury the castle of Devizes originally seized by Stephen in 1139; and he undertook to give land of equivalent value to Lincoln Cathedral if Ranulf of Chester failed to honour his promises over compensation for war damage. He thus hardly set a foot wrong, gave the bishops good reason to trust him, and ensured that at Stephen's court their demands for peace grew ever more insistent.

Finally, when Stephen and Henry met at Winchester on 6 November, Henry made it possible for churchmen and other moderates to give him their full endorsement by formally accepting that, in exchange for confirmation of his own rights of succession, Stephen should remain king for life. He also agreed to a general restoration of all estates unlawfully seized since 1135, thus soothing remaining fears about the security of magnate inheritances. In 1141 Matilda did not know when and how to bend, with the fatal result that too few felt they had a vested interest in the success of her cause. In 1153 it was Henry's great achievement that he met the needs of the time by conducting himself as neither a conqueror nor a usurper but as a worthy heir to the throne, anxious for peace, reconciliation and political unity.

In April 1154 Henry left England for Normandy. After Stephen's death at Dover on 25 October, six weeks passed before he returned to assume his inheritance. Haste was unnecessary. Only twenty-one years old on his coronation day, 19 December, he was the first king of England since the Conquest to succeed to the throne unopposed. Then, three years later, his recovery of the northern counties from Malcolm IV of Scotland marked the final stage in the passage of supremacy from the house of Blois to the house of Anjou.

# 4

# Royal government in England

Generally speaking, the twelfth century saw a rapid expansion of English royal government, particularly in the crown's capacity to control the localities directly and in detail. Stephen's reign was a very obvious exception to these centralising trends. Traditional interpretations stress problems of magnate oppression and rampant disorder, and that an end to the 'anarchy' came about only through Henry II's work of reconstruction after 1154. These interpretations, however, draw heavily on the alarmist writings of the chroniclers, and there was a notable discrepancy between the total collapse of government they perceived and what happened in reality.

Despite much dislocation, at no point in the reign did orderly royal rule break down completely. Warfare clearly posed the gravest threat to it, but less of a threat than we have been led to believe. Truly large-scale fighting was not often seen in England in the 1140s and early 1150s, and the relative stagnation of the hostilities after 1141 saw the consolidation of a northern region ruled by King David, a western region ruled by Empress Matilda, and an eastern region ruled by King Stephen. Historians have often found it difficult to come to terms with this situation, as if the fragmentation of crown authority was merely another sign of endemic instability. But there is no denying that David and Matilda brought the main war theatres under more or less stable control, and just as they ensured that a substantial part of

England was subject to royal government after 1141, so did Stephen. The areas that now suffered most from the fighting were the 'frontier' counties (for example, Berkshire and Wiltshire) between Stephen's and Matilda's respective heartlands. Elsewhere, major midland rebellions erupted in 1143–4 (Geoffrey de Mandeville) and 1146–7 (Ranulf of Chester); but there are reasons, dealt with later (pp. 70–1, 79–84), for believing that many bishops and magnates worked to uphold local peace, and that helped to compensate for the inadequacies of royal control wherever it was weak. Even when Stephen's fortunes crashed in 1141, therefore, the consequences were not all harmful to the state of the country.

Since royal government in the names of David and Matilda has already been considered, this chapter will concentrate on Stephen's administration both before and after the watershed year of 1141. It is also concerned exclusively with secular government; Stephen's dealings with the English Church are discussed in chapter 5.

## King Stephen's government, 1135–40

It is impossible to accept the familiar argument that Stephen irresponsibly neglected or mismanaged his duty to govern England. On the old and still influential interpretation, his decision in 1139 to arrest the experienced viceroy, Bishop Roger of Salisbury, was seen as an administrative catastrophe precipitating 'anarchy' – it destroyed Henry I's governmental machine and forced Stephen to make dangerous concessions to the magnates, whereas Henry had been careful to repress them by governing through his own officials. But there are good grounds why that analysis should be revised. Recent work by the Japanese historian Kenji Yoshitake (1988a) has underlined that Roger's removal had no serious impact on routine royal administration. Another powerful reason for questioning the old view is that it rests on the false notion that the only satisfactory form of medieval government was a highly centralised one. Stephen, in brief, had a practical approach to kingship. This involved a deliberate shift in administrative policy which automatically reduced Roger's importance; that does not seem to have been planned from the beginning (despite a recent argument to the contrary (Warren 1987: 93–4)), but grew out of the need to prop up a system unable to cope with the abnormal pressures imposed on it. Thus it can be argued that, far from foolishly jeopardising royal authority, Stephen had a good understanding of government and took sensible steps to try to stabilise the realm.

At first, though, government did continue along the lines laid down by Henry I. Notably in the key areas of finance and justice, royal government under Henry had become more elaborate, more interventionist, and more demanding. The main innovations were the appearance of a chief minister (Bishop Roger), responsible for the kingdom's management, especially while Henry was absent in France, the introduction of the exchequer for strict central auditing of crown revenue, and the recruitment of a large body of professional royal servants who, as sheriffs and visiting justices, carried the king's authority directly into the shires. Few of these men belonged to wealthy families, and if necessary they could be used to keep troublesome magnates in check. It was, however, not so much fear of 'overmighty' subjects as the increasing complexity of government that caused Henry to turn to the lesser nobility, for they could supply the practical bureaucratic skills then more vital in governing England than the great lords' military resources and expertise. And even so, as C. Warren Hollister (1986) and Judith Green (1986) have stressed, the magnates were still closely involved in royal rule – not least in shire government which, for all the advances made by central power, depended for its smooth working on the active cooperation of these 'natural' leaders of the local communities. Thus, although by 1135 a new balance had begun to be struck between magnates and bureaucrats, the growth of state authority was not dictated by anti-magnate policies. Indeed, the chief reason for it was Henry's concern to squeeze money from England in order to finance his wars in France. Stephen himself began by retaining many of the personnel employed by Henry I, and Bishop Roger kept his position at the head of the administration. But even before his disgrace in 1139, Roger, and the kind of government he stood for, did not meet Stephen's requirements, and a radical administrative restructuring was already underway.

Unlike Henry I, Stephen did not rule a unified England and had in addition to cope with acute problems of national defence.

The Henrician system could not keep order, or even guarantee adequate war finance. It followed that government had to change, and it was therefore essentially the impact of emergency wartime needs that interrupted the pattern of administrative development. One obvious discontinuity arose from the fact that on Stephen's return from Normandy in November 1137 the defence of his position in England committed him to being a resident king. That meant he had less need of a chief minister, and Bishop Roger's importance was correspondingly diminished, so that he may have been in virtual retirement when arrested. (In any event, he was then in his seventies and a sick man, with little left to contribute.) Government thus managed without him in part because the central administration had already been brought more directly under Stephen's personal supervision. Two interrelated changes were even more basic, and served only to confirm Roger's irrelevance. Whereas Henry I had ceased to rely quite so heavily on the magnates in running the kingdom, under Stephen this trend was reversed; and whereas Henry had increased central control over the localities, there was now, in W.L. Warren's phrase, 'a shift of executive power from the centre to the provinces' (1987: 93).

The point that needs to be developed first is that Stephen quickly began to direct affairs primarily in consultation with soldier-administrators. These persons were senior members of the royal military household – the magnates who, as the king's war captains, were most closely associated with the defence of the throne. According to the assessment of their pre-1135 role in Anglo-Norman politics by J.O. Prestwich, such men 'enjoyed the confidence of the king, shared in his counsels and judgments and stood at the centre of power, jealously guarding their privileges and opportunities' (1981: 16). Under Stephen this military element unsurprisingly gained even greater prominence. They certainly resented Bishop Roger's lingering influence and put pressure on Stephen to arrest him. But it is unfortunate that this episode has normally been interpreted purely in terms of factional politics. One problem with that approach is that Stephen was too shrewd simply to have been manipulated by worthless favourites. In any case, that description hardly applies to the magnates concerned, for they were men of some integrity. Again, since warfare was their business they were understandably dismayed by Roger's refusal to accept the primacy of military over other considerations (p. 20), while the accusation that he had embezzled royal revenues, even if untrue, probably reflected genuine anxieties about inadequate war finance. All this suggests that the magnates, while wishing to consolidate their hold at the centre of power, were also concerned for the interests of the crown, and believed that they were better equipped to serve the country's needs than royal bureaucrats familiar only with peacetime administration. It is not difficult to see why Stephen relied on them and why, as was appropriate in a national emergency, the king and his military leaders, an experienced 'war cabinet', took overall charge of the realm's affairs.

Yet more remarkable was the decentralisation of government to the regions. Henry I had created hardly any new earldoms, and most (only seven existed in 1135) were treated as honorific dignities. By contrast, as R.H.C. Davis (1990: 125ff.) and Paul Latimer (1986) have shown, Stephen created no fewer than twelve new earldoms between 1138 and 1140, and a significant number of earls had their authority reinforced by special grants of official powers, normally within the shires of their own earldoms. At their widest, these grants comprised all the king's rights in the county concerned, so that the earl, effectively a regional viceroy, took charge of finance, justice and military resources, treated the sheriff as his deputy, and in general assumed overall responsibility for peace-keeping and for re-inforcing royal authority in his area. Thus, new power structures emerged, based on the notion of military-administrative earldoms or provincial governorships.

This reversal of Henry I's centralising policies has been seen as a serious blow to royal power on the grounds that Stephen weakly allowed ambitious magnates to cash in on his difficulties and become too powerful and independent. Behind this lies the assumption that the local interests of great families were always a menace to the crown and never an asset. Yet this ignores the point already made that magnate power had complemented bureaucratic power and played a vital part in upholding Henry I's authority. Of course, magnates were anxious to increase their local prominence, and so private ambitions did help to shape Stephen's policy; nor was it without *potential* dangers. But, for one thing, Stephen needed to give key men a vested interest in his cause by increasing their local authority and prestige; for another, since the problems of controlling the kingdom were overstretching the resources of central power, he had to have more help from the magnates than Henry I had needed. In the circumstances, it was therefore a necessary response to increase their local effectiveness by granting them special powers as regional governors and, if they carried out their duties properly, the king and his household could concentrate on the most pressing needs of national defence. The latest research indicates that none of Stephen's new earldoms appeared earlier than 1138, a year of major Scottish invasions and mounting internal unrest. This supports the conclusion that he was acting constructively to stabilise royal power in difficult times. In fact, William of Malmesbury linked the creation of new earls with the rebellion of Robert of Gloucester, whose defection in 1138 threw the West Country into open revolt (Potter 1955: 23).

That Stephen was adopting a sensible strategy is reinforced by other evidence. The earls he appointed were often his most reliable and capable supporters, comrades in arms like his son-in-law, Hervey Brito, earl of Wiltshire, 'a man of distinction and soldierly qualities' according to the *Gesta Stephani* (Potter 1976: 109). It is also highly significant that earls were normally given control of shire government only in those vulnerable areas where they needed strong powers to police their districts effectively. Such provincial governors included, besides Hervey Brito, Alan of Brittany (Cornwall), William le Gros (Yorkshire), and Waleran of Meulan (Worcester), all of whom were entrusted with strategically vital regions. A good earlier parallel is found in the regalian rights given by William the Conqueror to the marcher earls of Northumberland, Chester, Shrewsbury and Hereford, obviously to equip them for the task of controlling insecure frontier districts. Conversely, in more stable zones Stephen's earls usually had few official powers. In such cases, Stephen normally retained most of his royal rights, including control of the sheriffs, and this underlines the responsible nature of his policy. Moreover, he never intended to give any earl a completely free hand. All were seen as public officers answerable to the crown, and since it was Stephen's preference to favour those who were leading members of the military household, that in itself helped to uphold the crown's direct authority in the regions. There was thus an extensive but not uncontrolled delegation of royal power. Clearly, however, the long-term success of Stephen's policy was going to depend on one very important consideration: his ability to retain magnate confidence and loyalty. But what if the war took a turn for the worse?

Before that happened in 1141, the Beaumonts were the most well-rewarded and successful of Stephen's earls, and their outstanding role in royal service shows just how productive the partnership between king and earls could be. The joint heads of the family in 1135 were the twin brothers Robert, earl of Leicester, and Waleran, count of Meulan (in the French Vexin, between Normandy and Paris). As great cross-Channel magnates, they had been major forces in Henry I's reign, were closely connected with the Clares, the Warennes and other prominent families, and rapidly established themselves as Stephen's most important war captains. Waleran was largely responsible for upholding the king's authority in Normandy and delaying large-scale Angevin conquest there until 1141. In England, the Beaumonts and their main allies controlled three earldoms in 1135; in 1138 they held seven, half the number then in existence. Of these, Leicester, Northampton, Warwick and Waleran's new earldom of Worcester were used by Stephen in the late 1130s to guarantee the allegiance and good order of the Midlands. They formed, in David Crouch's words, 'a "Mercia" to set against the hostile "Wessex" that was being built up against him by Earl Robert of Gloucester' (1986: 41). The twins' pre-eminence in government was confirmed when Stephen struck against Bishop Roger, whose arrest they strongly supported. But although Stephen's preferential treatment of the Beaumonts has been firmly condemned as rash, they were able to advance their interests only because he regarded their political weight and military skills as vital to the defence of the Anglo-Norman state. Indeed, had a different policy been adopted, it seems very likely that the early part of the reign would have been far more unstable than it actually was.

## King Stephen's government, 1141–53

Thus Stephen reformed his administration in an attempt to rule his war-torn kingdom more effectively. But his defeat and capture at Lincoln adversely affected the situation in two fundamental ways. First, on his release in November 1141 he regained some of his power; but Empress Matilda now ruled her western province in a royal manner, just as King David exercised sovereignty in the north. A high degree of stability could be achieved, with most of the north, for example, being ruled by David from Carlisle more effectively than it had ever been ruled from London. Nevertheless, three rival rulers were now exercising what had previously been the crown's monopoly rights over revenue, coinage and justice. That was a completely unprecedented situation, and Stephen's efforts to govern on a national scale had irretrievably broken down.

In the second place, due to the failure of Stephen's unifying leadership in both England and Normandy he could no longer rely on the active cooperation of the earls. He lost his greatest assets when the Beaumonts were forced to reconsider their positions: Count Waleran reluctantly joined the Angevins in the autumn of 1141 to safeguard his extensive continental estates; Earl Robert withdrew from the dynastic struggle to concentrate on his own concerns. Although most earls continued to recognise Stephen as king, many (like Earl Robert) withdrew their active support and appeared at court rarely or not at all. Thus personal contact with the centre was lost. The earls became more independent than Stephen had ever intended, and they consolidated their regional strength with scant regard for crown interests. A period of anarchy did not ensue, for as their grip tightened, so disorder was prevented from getting entirely out of hand. But although Stephen's administrative policies had been working well, once the war began to go badly they had the unintended effect of seriously damaging the crown. Decentralisation went too far.

As a result of these developments, the scope and effectiveness of Stephen's authority were much reduced after 1141. But equally evident is the resilience with which his much-maligned government coped with the new situation. The king and his household strove with some success to maintain continuity in central administration: the chancery (secretariat) continued to function; exchequer sessions were still held; and royal justice was dispensed in the shires. Written administration, a vital aspect of government, arguably experienced the least deterioration. Henry I issued for England and Normandy nearly 1,500 surviving charters during his thirty-five-year reign; Stephen issued about 730, executed to the same high standard, during his much shorter nineteen-year reign. It has been calculated by Edward Kealey (1974) that as high a proportion as 52 per cent were issued in 1135–42, and that the average annual rate of production decreased sharply after 1140. But if the written output dwindled, so did the territory Stephen ruled and the number of petitioners who regarded his charters as good security for their lands and rights. There is, therefore, no question but that Stephen's government continued to discharge written tasks efficiently.

What the charters also show is that after 1141 Stephen exercised some kind of authority across virtually the length and breadth of eastern England, which contained most of the shires and main towns and the majority of bishoprics and monasteries. But within this truncated realm, his administration was most active in the south-east, which may be called Stephen's 'inner' zone. For example, no less than 74 per cent of Stephen's charters which have place-dates for the period 1142–53 were issued at London, clearly his administrative headquarters, or within 60 miles of the city. Outside the south-east, in Stephen's 'outer' zone, government depended largely on the earls, into whose areas he rarely came and who thus lacked regular support from the centre, and were less accountable to it.

This notion of two eastern zones, with Stephen's government strong in the one and much weaker in the other, is supported by recent studies, especially the important work by Edmund King (1984) and Graeme White (1985). These concern, first, the records relating to the Danegeld (land tax) levied by Henry II in 1156. Full accounts survive for twenty-nine counties, and they were systematically analysed as long ago as 1903 to establish the percentages of the shire assessments written off due to 'waste'. The resultant findings were thought to point to prolonged fighting and widespread devastation in the 1140s and early 1150s, especially in the Midlands. But new arguments have indicated that the term 'waste' stood simply for land making no return of tax, and that the sums excused reflect not so much war damage (though this had clearly occurred) as the administrative difficulties Henry had inherited due to inadequate financial records, tax-evasion and unresolved property disputes.

Now, four of the six shires with the highest percentages of 'waste' had been on Stephen's western frontier. In Oxfordshire (39 per cent) and Berkshire (38 per cent), where Angevin strongpoints had defied the king, two rival jurisdictions had repeatedly clashed and stable government could not be maintained in Stephen's name. Similar were the effects in Warwickshire (63 per cent) and Leicestershire (51 per cent), where the earls could not be relied on to uphold royal interests. But the key point is that six of the nine shires with the lowest percentages of 'waste' had been Stephen's, four of which lay in the south-east – Surrey (17 per cent), Middlesex (12 per cent), Sussex (4 per cent) and Kent (0.4 per cent). There, it seems clear, records were kept up to date, evasions of tax were less common, and disputes over land were less numerous. And that provides some telling evidence for relatively good administrative order within Stephen's heartland.

Work on Stephen's exchequer and coinage tells much the same story (King 1984; Yoshitake 1988b; Boon 1988). In the home counties, the exchequer still functioned, and its control over the collection of crown revenues was reasonably strong; royal mints, notably those at Colchester and London itself, operated efficiently. Indeed, it almost goes without saying that Stephen's prolonged war effort could hardly have been sustained without significant degrees of successful management in these crucial contexts. In the outer zone, however, central control was much patchier. Some earls retained royal revenues for themselves rather than accounting for them at the exchequer; and Stephen was left without much authority over the mint towns, some of which issued coins struck from local rather than centrally authorised dies.

So from 1141 Stephen's government was regional rather than national, and even within its region it operated under obvious strains. But in London and the south-east his control probably did not differ very markedly from that of Henry I. In the early 1150s this area was run directly on Stephen's behalf by men like Richard de Lucy, justice of London, Middlesex and Essex, and William Martel, sheriff of Surrey and the head of the royal household. (De Lucy's administrative ability would be recognised by Henry II, who in 1168 made him justiciar of England.) In the outer zone, crown authority depended on the nature of Stephen's relations with individual earls, and royal government was not uniformly upheld. There were two main reasons why the earls' activities might undermine it. On the one hand, some cynically took advantage of infrequent royal supervision to manipulate local government entirely for their own ends. On the other, if earls could not rely on regular support from the centre, they had to safeguard their power bases as best they could, and that naturally involved putting their own interests first. Central control was not essential to local stability. But when the earls enforced peace, as many of them did, it was their peace rather than the king's, and frequent complaints were made about their high-handed conduct. There was little hope of redress by appealing to the crown and, in particular, Stephen's inability to ensure that the rule of law was impartially upheld meant that in many local communities royal justice lost much of its authority and respect.

Yet while there were clear limits on what Stephen's government could achieve outside the south-east, the distinction between inner and outer zones should not be *too* sharply drawn. John of Hexham, a northern chronicler, reports that in 1142 Stephen restored peace between the earls of Richmond and York; that in 1148 the revenues of the archbishopric of York were paid into the king's treasury; and that in 1149 Stephen imposed fines on the men of Beverley and levied taxes from the citizens of York. The earl of York himself was Stephen's cousin William le Gros, and though his actions sometimes troubled the king (Dalton 1990), he maintained an alert defence against the Scots, played a vital role in upholding crown rights during the protracted struggle over the York archbishopric (pp. 65–6), and dutifully reported back to Stephen in the 1140s at Northampton, London and Canterbury. Moreover, just as the crown's right to requisition castles at will was enforced against the earl of Essex in 1143, so it was against the earl of Chester in 1146; and just as the earl of Essex was treated as a removable public officer in 1143, so was the earl of Lincoln in 1149. In such ways Stephen upheld himself as the ultimate authority throughout his region, and the principle that earldoms were subject to the crown was never entirely lost.


### The reassertion of monarchical authority, 1154–7


Henry II's undisputed succession on Stephen's death removed the reasons for the administrative changes and dislocation of his predecessor's reign, and the development of centralised kingship was swiftly resumed. It was Henry's declared policy to re-establish the 'good government' of his grandfather, Henry I, as if Stephen's reign had no redeeming features at all. To be sure, the new king had to take a very firm grip of royal justice and finance. Yet again, though no one doubted Henry's right to rule, in parts of England real power lay with the magnates rather than the crown, and a more acceptable balance had to be struck. Finally, the Scots continued to govern the north, and did not withdraw to the Tweed–Solway line until 1157. Only then were the traditions of English monarchy and a united kingdom restored.

On the other hand, however, in reviving royal power Henry had scarcely to begin from scratch, and his difficulties, though grave, must not be overstated – after all, the speed with which he achieved results is very striking. In the west, Henry's problems were lightened by Matilda's efforts to uphold royal government; in the north, he could build on King David's successes, which probably made this area more governable than it had been in 1135. But Henry's greatest advantage – and the real reason why crown authority was so rapidly revived after 1154 – was Stephen's staunch defence of his royal rights to the limits of his power. That point, of course, applies particularly strongly to the south-east. But nor should it be ignored that once peace had returned in 1153 Stephen acted vigorously to recover some of his lost authority. In the treaty of Westminster, he insisted that he should rule 'in the whole realm of England, both in the duke's part and in my own'. The best evidence that these were more than empty words is provided by Stephen's new coinage of 1153–4. Struck from official, London-made dies and issued at no fewer than thirty-eight mints (including former Angevin strongholds like Gloucester and Hereford), it represented a determined and largely successful attempt to restore the crown's control over coining. Thus, concludes Graeme White, in his work of reconstruction Henry II was 'in some respects . . . continuing what Stephen had begun' (1990: 20), which serves only to underline that the damage done to royal government in Stephen's reign was not as disastrous as has often been supposed.

# 5
# King Stephen and the English Church

The support of the higher clergy was as crucial as that of the magnates for the stability of royal power. The context for Stephen's dealings with the English Church is set, however, not only by the war of succession, but by the far-reaching claims of the revived twelfth-century papacy, which sought to bind the 'regional Churches' of western Christendom in strict obedience to Rome. To the Angevin and Scottish assaults on Stephen's kingship was thus added the threat posed by the expansionist policies of a *third* major foreign power. Vital royal interests were no less at risk, for the papacy wished to free English churchmen as far as was possible from secular rule and involvement, despite the crown's need to control the allegiance of all its subjects. Custom was of course against papal claims, and was all the stronger for its being rooted in a centuries-old tradition of mutually beneficial cooperation, with the crown as master providing endowments and protection, and the higher clergy as its servants offering administrative expertise and their loyal support as great landowners. Yet in the Constitutions of Clarendon (1164), Henry II took the unprecedented step of formally reasserting royal authority over the English Church by imposing written conditions on it. What had happened to crown–church relations in Stephen's reign?

Traditionally, this period has been seen as a fundamental turning-point, in that for the first time English churchmen were brought into regular contact with Rome and systematically opposed lay intervention in ecclesiastical affairs. Thus, royal control of the Church and clerical loyalties apparently broke down completely and, here as elsewhere, few historians have looked far beyond Stephen's 'mismanagement' for their explanations. His biggest mistake, it has been thought, was the arrest of the bishops (Roger of Salisbury and Alexander of Lincoln) in 1139, for that forced the Church to withdraw support, accelerated papal centralisation, and ultimately prevented the king from securing his royal line with Eustace's coronation. Yet, as Frank Barlow (1979) and others have argued, the course of events was in large measure determined by the unfavourable nature of Henry I's legacy, by rapid developments in papal government and, not least, by the abnormal circumstances of the reign itself. It is also dangerous to assume that the loss of royal authority, though serious, was as complete as Henry II's reaction suggests. Due allowance made, Stephen in fact did not do badly in defending his rights, just as was the case in secular government. Furthermore, despite obvious tensions, there is no evidence to support the idea of a sustained rift in crown–church relations. Political stability was the main aim of the higher clergy, and even when, in 1152–3, their opposition to Stephen's policies became critical, concern to restore peace to the realm eclipsed any desire to gain greater freedom from the crown, which they respected and, within limits, dutifully served. After all, as a group they showed an impressive degree of loyalty to Stephen personally, helped him through some major crises, and upheld him as king for life.

## King Stephen's ecclesiastical policy

Even before Stephen's accession, a new era in English church history had already begun, one characterised by compromise and adjustment between royal and papal claims. Henry I's reluctant surrender in 1107 of the right to invest bishops and abbots with ring and pastoral staff, the symbols of spiritual authority, had weakened the crown's position, and although in practice Henry retained wide powers, especially in the vital matter of ecclesiastical appointments, the ground was nevertheless prepared for a more independent English Church. Thus, as M. Brett has stressed, by Henry's death the principle had been firmly established that the crown no longer had exclusive claims on the clergy's allegiance; papal intervention in England had become routine; and a new generation of bishops 'conceived of the liberty of the Church in a . . . more urgent sense' (1975: 112). This, then, was the difficult situation confronting Stephen in 1135, and he came under immediate pressure to make further concessions. His promise to relax royal controls was necessary to secure his coronation and his recognition by Pope Innocent II, and at Oxford in April 1136 he issued a charter of liberties for the Church. But he did not, as some historians have supposed, simply capitulate to the reformers and strip himself of power. Much of the 'Oxford' charter was fairly standard; key clauses concerning ecclesiastical jurisdiction and vacant bishoprics were left deliberately imprecise; and of utmost significance was the king's final statement: 'All this I grant and confirm, saving my royal and rightful dignity.' Thus, while recognising that a measure of reform was necessary, Stephen reserved the customary royal prerogative to interpret church liberty at pleasure and keep it in bounds. And that was a sensible attempt to strike a balance between the importance of retaining clerical support and the need to preserve crown rights.

But three major interlocking factors impeded the long-term success of Stephen's policy. None of the most basic royal rights of management, as later defined at Clarendon, were allowed to lapse entirely. These were: the exercise of important jurisdictional powers; control of vacant bishoprics and royal abbeys; influence over church appointments; requirement of homage and fealty from bishops and greater abbots as tenants-in-chief of the crown; restrictions on contact with Rome. But their systematic enforcement was obviously compromised by the crown's growing weakness. For instance, as royal justice foundered, so the church courts extended their jurisdiction at the crown's expense, and appeals to Rome for final judicial decisions became more frequent. In the second place, a new European-wide upsurge in reform gave fresh impetus to papal imperialism and further eroded the royal position. The Cistercians, under the forceful guidance of St Bernard of Clairvaux, stood at the forefront of the twelfth-century reform movement; they had close links with the papacy, opposed royal supervision of their affairs, and were especially successful in England, where they controlled some fifty abbeys by 1154. Furthermore, Master Gratian of Bologna's highly influential *Decretum* (*c.* 1140), a landmark in the history of papal government, clarified the law of the Church (canon law), strengthened the pope's judicial supremacy, and made the priesthood throughout western Europe more aware of its rights and duties. Admittedly, copies of the *Decretum* did not circulate in England much earlier than 1150, and it is important not to overestimate the influence that even the mighty St Bernard had over English affairs (Holdsworth 1986). But by a natural process the English higher clergy were becoming more familiar with papal monarchy in action, more conscious of their privileged status, and more ready to question royal demands.

Finally, Stephen's third main difficulty was that as warfare intensified, so his church policy hardened, not because he cynically broke his promises (as some historians have concluded), but because during national emergencies he and his war captains naturally expected the clergy to put royal needs first. When he punished churchmen who refused to cooperate – the arrest of the bishops in 1139 being the classic example – his position, as he saw it, was totally defensible according to customary royal practices and the terms of his charter of 1136. But although conflict never got completely out of hand (as happened during Henry II's struggle with Thomas Becket), such actions were bound to damage the crown's standing with both the pope and the English Church to a degree scarcely imaginable a generation or so earlier. Related to this was the fact that Stephen's insecurity not only forced him to stress traditional royal rights, but prevented him from reducing their offensiveness by providing the compensations of peace and public order that Henry I's strong rule had offered. All told, therefore, it says much for Stephen's staunch defence of the royal position, and the higher clergy's restraint, that the crown's central place in ecclesiastical affairs was not wholly forfeited.

Stephen attended English church councils to try to control them, or else sent along his agents to uphold royal rights. He had successes in restricting the clergy's contact with papal envoys and the pope himself. Legates from Rome who entered England without his consent were expelled, and there was only one legatine mission of any importance, Alberic of Ostia's in 1138-9. Merely five bishops were allowed to attend the Second

Lateran Council (1139); three were licensed to answer Eugenius III's general summons to the council of Rheims (1148), and Archbishop Theobald of Canterbury was the only English churchman to take part without Stephen's permission. Most crucial, however, was the question of ecclesiastical appointments. Senior churchmen controlled important estates and military resources, and the disputed succession placed a premium on Stephen's ability to ensure that such assets were in safe hands. Early in the reign, four of Stephen's kinsmen gained office in strategically vital areas: his illegitimate son, Gervase, became abbot of Westminster, his cousin, Robert, abbot of Winchcombe in Gloucestershire, his nephew, Hugh, abbot of St Benet of Hulme in Norfolk, and another nephew, William fitz Herbert, archbishop of York. It is nonetheless clear that Stephen failed to retain a strong grip on church patronage. Despite occasional royal successes, the clergy normally controlled appointments to major abbeys from c. 1140, and appointments to bishoprics from c. 1143.

The result was that, by the late 1140s and early 1150s, the higher clergy had been infiltrated to an unprecedented extent by men who were not crown appointees and were often conscientious reformers. And yet the threat to Stephen's authority must not be overstated. One important point is that free canonical elections did not necessarily involve the choice of candidates unacceptable to the king. The most revealing example is provided by Hugh du Puiset, another royal nephew, who became bishop of Durham canonically in 1153. Very instructive in a different way is the case of the archbishopric of York, a vital northern bastion which Stephen naturally wanted to secure for his own man. William fitz Herbert was accordingly forced on the electors in 1141, but he was bitterly opposed by the Cistercians in Yorkshire and by St Bernard. Eventually (though not until 1147) William was deposed by the Cistercian pope Eugenius III and replaced by the Cistercian abbot of Fountains, St Bernard's friend Henry Murdac – an obvious instance of Rome's increasing influence over the English Church to the detriment of the crown. On the face of it, this was also a clear-cut, if belated, victory for the reformers; but in fact no party, least of all the Church, profited from this turn of events. Stephen understandably refused to recognise Henry Murdac as the new archbishop, and he retained enough influence over church affairs to confiscate York's lands and bar Murdac from York for three years. In other words, if he could not keep his own man in, he could keep the pope's man out. Then, after Murdac's death in October 1153, representations were made to the new pope, Anastasius IV, and William fitz Herbert was reinstated. So, as Stephen's reign drew to its close, both Durham and York were held by royal nephews, and that in itself is a good reason for caution when assessing how far crown control over the Church had been lost.

## Conflict and stability

More can be learned about crown–church relations from Stephen's dealings with his two greatest prelates: Henry of Winchester and Theobald of Canterbury. Both exploited the king's difficulties to extend clerical rights, and Theobald, after emerging from Henry's shadow in 1143, ultimately held greater political authority than any English churchman had previously enjoyed. Accounts of their careers, however, have often placed an unfortunate stress on the stormier side of their relationship with the crown. A more balanced approach shows that neither was totally committed to overturning the status quo, that such an attitude was characteristic of the higher clergy as a whole, and that, in general, the Church was an important force for political stability.

Though Bishop Henry was Stephen's brother, and had played a key role in securing his coronation, he was also the pope's personal representative as resident legate for England (1139–43) and a staunch supporter of church reform. When the bishops were arrested in 1139 he thus took his stand as a champion of church liberty against royal abuse of the clergy. Yet Kenji Yoshitake's recent study (1988a) has at last firmly disposed of the view that on this issue the Church broke with the crown. At his first legatine council, which began at Winchester on 29 August 1139, Henry insisted that Stephen be called to account under canon law. The Church, however, did not present a united front at this council; nor was Henry himself prepared to carry his defence of clerical rights to the point of an open breach with the king. He suspended proceedings without condemning Stephen and (with Archbishop Theobald) begged him, William of Malmesbury tells us, 'not to suffer a divorce to be made between the monarchy and the clergy' (Potter 1955: 34) – a striking demonstration that, however distressed they were, church leaders still wanted reasonable relations with the king. Thus, paradoxically, the crisis of 1139 serves to highlight the basic interdependence of Church and crown rather than the divisions between them.

In the main Stephen, for all his insecurity, also tried not to go too far. In 1138 he had accepted Theobald's free election to Canterbury with good grace, aware no doubt that Canterbury was specially privileged and that not even Henry I had dared to dictate appointments to this see (Barlow 1979: 82). In 1139 Stephen was careful to punish the bishops as disloyal barons, depriving them not of their bishoprics but only of their castles, and that was acceptable to Archbishop Hugh of Rouen, who openly took the king's side. The dramatic events of 1141 also drive home the desire of both parties to avoid outright confrontation. Alexander of Lincoln, despite his treatment in 1139, celebrated mass for the royal army before the battle of Lincoln. After Stephen's capture, the Church had to submit to Empress Matilda; but Theobald and most bishops accepted her only after they had made their distaste at abandoning an anointed king abundantly plain (p. 42). The year then ended with a formal reconciliation between king and Church, for both saw the importance of renewing relations as speedily as possible.

Thereafter, indeed, Henry usually cooperated with Stephen. For his part, Theobald was even more strongly committed to church reform, but he too believed that clerical interests were normally best served by maintaining a working relationship with the crown. It is true that he defied Stephen to attend the papal council of Rheims: royal agents seized Canterbury's lands in retaliation; Theobald was sent into exile; and so in 1148 the king, far from being powerless, excluded *both* his archbishops from their sees. But, once again, the repercussions should not be overstressed. Theobald showed his basic reverence for royal authority by preventing Eugenius III from excommunicating Stephen, which would have not only shattered the bond between Church and king but freed *all* Stephen's subjects from their oaths of allegiance. Instead an interdict was laid on England; even then, most bishops supported the crown and refused to suspend religious services. Next, Theobald sought a settlement with Stephen, and much was excused on either side. It is also significant that, before his return to England, Theobald had consecrated Gilbert Foliot, a partisan of Empress Matilda, as bishop of Hereford only after Foliot's promise to give allegiance to Stephen, because (as Theobald insisted) 'a bishop had no right to cause schism within the Church by refusing fealty to the prince approved by the papacy'.

There are, therefore, real dangers of exaggerating what church liberty actually meant in practice, even when royal power was in retreat. Because his armoury still contained concrete sanctions like forfeiture and banishment, Stephen retained a significant measure of control. Furthermore, reforming bishops realistically accepted that the crown must have some rights over the Church. Accordingly, they recognised a dual allegiance to pope and king, tried to serve both masters – however difficult that might be – and drew back from all-out clashes that would only harm Church and crown alike. In turn, Stephen protected himself by acting with as much restraint as circumstances allowed; and this mutual concern to ease as far as possible the real tensions that existed, and to keep on cooperating, brought to Stephen's troubled reign a greater sense of orderliness than would otherwise have been the case.

But on one basic issue there was no room for compromise. Thus in April 1152 Theobald led the English Church in an unprecedented display of united opposition to the crown and categorically refused to anoint Eustace as Stephen's successor. What had caused this crisis? Eugenius III's personal rejection of Stephen's proposals for Eustace's coronation has sometimes given the impression that the bishops simply closed ranks against the king as submissive servants of a powerful pope, who was enraged by Stephen's treatment of the archbishops in 1148. But, in essence, their opposition had little directly to do with deference to papal authority, or any desire for greater ecclesiastical freedom; nor is it clear (as has been argued) that Stephen could have avoided this defeat if he had handled Anglo–papal relations differently. Theobald's mind was already made up, and his central purpose was to end the war of succession. Only in that sense was there a real crisis in crown–church relations during Stephen's reign; and since behind it there lay clerical concern for the welfare of the realm (and continued willingness to safeguard Stephen's position as king), it reinforces the view that, by and large, the Church was committed to stability and order.

Stephen, like any secular ruler, saw his dynasty's survival as vital to the 'national interest', while Theobald looked to the well-being of the Church and the kingdom. The basic royal duty, as Theobald saw it, was to secure peace and protect the Church. He accepted that war might be morally defensible, but only if fought for the general good, and in reaching this judgement, Theobald and his advisers were undoubtedly influenced by the teachings of canonists and theologians on the notion of the 'just war'. Behind the authoritative definition to be found in Master Gratian's *Decretum* (Russell 1975) was St Augustine's familiar maxim that 'war is for the sake of peace' – an argument used by Henry I's supporters to justify his conquest of Normandy in 1106. There was, in other words, no such thing as a just war that did more harm than good. Given the deadlocked military situation in England, it followed that churchmen were duty-bound to oppose the king's dynastic policies, for Eustace's succession threatened to prolong indefinitely a war no one seemed capable of winning and which was therefore senseless and unjust.

But the decisive issue for Theobald was unquestionably the harsh reality that protracted and inconclusive war gravely damaged the Church. This, in turn, prevented Stephen from promoting the righteousness of his cause, the more so because wartime excesses, however justified by military necessity, were also committed in his name. Moreover, Stephen's reluctance to negotiate with his enemies also tested the clergy's loyalty to the full. Thus, in *c.* 1148 the author of the *Gesta Stephani* criticised Stephen and Matilda alike for their reckless pride, and complained that, far from wanting to end the kingdom's misfortunes, 'both parties courted strife' (Potter 1976: 187). In brief, warfare had got out of hand, did not coerce the wicked as just wars should, and had turned the crown itself into an oppressor of the clergy.

Admittedly, it has been stressed by Thomas Callahan (1974) that only about 10 per cent of all English religious houses are specifically known to have sustained material losses between 1135 and 1154. In addition, an exceptionally large number of new monasteries were founded during the reign – on one estimate, at least 120 houses. But while these points help to

69

modify the traditional picture of widespread disorder, the Church still took the brunt of warfare and the lawlessness it fostered, and the fact remains that sacrilege was being perpetrated on a totally unacceptable scale. As a matter of course, the hostilities involved the fortification or destruction of stone-built churches and general harrying of the countryside. Again, because of the crown's weakness, there was little to stop powerful magnates from expanding their influence by taking church land or by imposing arbitrary taxation; and magnate feuds occasionally erupted into violence, with further damage to the Church and its interests.

Indeed, the scourge of war caused all manner of problems for the higher clergy and orderly religious life. Many bishops were also alarmed about the moral and physical welfare of their flocks, and they recognised that as long as a state of emergency existed, Stephen was likely to take a firm line against clerical privileges. Disunity in the realm also encouraged disunity in the Church for, without a strong king, administrative shortcomings and rivalries were heightened and there was a real risk of schism. Yet again, war intensified the problem of worldly entanglements and retarded spiritual reform of the clergy. Even senior churchmen were themselves in moral peril. As tenants-in-chief of the crown, they might be required to accompany their knights on campaign and advise on military matters. That was acceptable under canon law, provided they observed the canonical prohibitions on clerical bearing of arms and shedding of blood. But some bishops, notably ex-royal servants like Nigel of Ely, failed to reconcile their spiritual and secular roles and brought disgrace and hardship on the Church. As the *Gesta Stephani* put it: 'girt with swords and wearing magnificent suits of armour, [they] rode on horseback with the haughtiest destroyers of the country and took their share of the spoil' (Potter 1976: 157).

Theobald could hardly ignore such evils. In fact if some bishops behaved badly, others worked hard *throughout* the reign to limit oppression and strife – another reason for seeing the Church as an important stabilising force. In this, as Christopher Holdsworth (1987) has shown, they were naturally influenced by the so-called Peace and Truce of God developed by church authorities in France from *c*. 1000. The Truce of God banned hostilities at the most sacred times of the year, and (while there are clear examples to the contrary) the chroniclers of Stephen's reign sometimes mention lulls in the fighting in England during Lent or Advent. The Peace of God was intended to protect all non-combatants from violence and oppression, and the English church councils of 1138, 1143 and 1151 introduced tough sanctions in an attempt to bring offenders, especially the magnates, into line. Thus the Church, as Edmund King has stressed, was trying to fill the vacuum left by a crown unable to discharge its responsibilities. 'The weaker the central authority became', he concludes, 'the more important it became . . . to circumscribe the *potestas* [power] of the magnates' (King 1984: 134–5). Similarly, churchmen promoted peace by helping to arrange or reinforce truces and non-aggression pacts, as when the bishop of Lincoln guaranteed the famous agreement between the earls of Chester and Leicester in *c.* 1150.

Thanks to such efforts, disorder was less of a problem than it might have been. Obviously, though, they scarcely went far enough, and the only effective way to protect the Church, as Theobald fully realised, was to restore peace to the whole kingdom. Henry of Winchester had himself sought a general political settlement as early as 1140; it was with the same goal that he tried to control Matilda in 1141 (pp. 42–4). But he was dragged into the civil war; his cathedral city became a battleground; and, although he helped to negotiate the peace of 1153, his reputation never really recovered. By contrast, the peaceful succession of Henry II in 1154 has been seen by Adrian Morey and C.N.L. Brooke as 'a victory . . . for Theobald's slow-moving diplomacy' (1965: 90). His credibility as a peacemaker rested on his success in gradually uniting the Church under him (partly by appointing like-minded bishops), in raising it above partisan divisions, and in fixing realistic terms for a settlement. Of course, the Church continued to uphold Stephen as the lawful king, and in principle Theobald still wanted to cooperate with the crown. But, equally clearly, he could not do so when Stephen placed family interests above the public good. In all probability, Theobald had always believed that a lasting peace rested on a dynastic compromise: consequently, Eustace's coronation had to be resisted at all costs. Stephen tried to get his way in April 1152 by intimidating the bishops, but he could not overcome their opposition, even in Theobald's absence (he had fled abroad). Such solidarity is very striking, and on Duke Henry's invasion in 1153 Theobald was able to exert the full pressure of a unified Church on both Stephen and Henry to accept terms. Then, finally, Theobald and the bishops undertook to enforce the treaty of Westminster with all the penalties at their disposal.

Overall, however, it is still possible to agree with the verdict that in church affairs Stephen did not give more ground than he had to. As Frank Barlow has commented, Henry II's 'ability . . . to recover most of the traditional royal position in the church was due to Stephen's tenacious defence' (1979: 304); and in general, while papal authority steadily increased, its limitations can clearly be seen. On the whole the English Church was a stabilising force, concerned with promoting harmony at both local and national levels. That is why it was normally loyal to Stephen, and why it united against him only to prevent an unacceptable prolongation of the war. For all these reasons, Stephen's reign was less of a watershed in the history of crown–church relations than traditional views have supposed. The independent political role taken by the bishops in 1152 was in essence forced on them by the crown's inability to perform its protective function, a development they had hardly welcomed. It underlined that the Church, lacking an effective means of self-defence, needed a strong king as the only guarantee of public order, and thus had the paradoxical effect of reinforcing the traditional identity of interests. Viewed in these terms, the real legacy of the reign lies not in the extremes of Becket's quarrel with Henry II, but in the more characteristic working compromise between the rights of the Church and the still extensive prerogatives of the crown. In short, the 'Anarchy' drove home the fundamental truth that no amount of ecclesiastical liberty was an adequate substitute for the benefits of royal strength, and that alone is sufficient reason not to exaggerate how far the English Church had gained its 'freedom' by 1154.

# 6
# King Stephen and the magnates

The other major body with which Stephen had to deal was of course the magnates. The political history of post-Conquest England used to be seen as a constant power struggle between the king and the higher nobility, whose respective interests were totally opposed. Henry I's centralising policies, it was thought, provoked an inevitable backlash, and while Stephen blundered, power-hungry magnates aimed at independence and generally threw the country into turmoil. Thus, civil war and the collapse of crown authority after 1135 were believed to have been caused by a potent mixture of baronial turbulence and royal ineptitude, and it was only Henry II's ability to tame the magnates that finally curbed 'feudal anarchy' and restored the status quo.

Although these older assumptions are still influential, perhaps nowhere has recent work on Norman England produced more basic reassessments than in this field of crown–magnate relations. The new approach stresses the basic interdependence of crown and magnates, a relationship very similar to that between crown and Church. The king relied on the magnates for military support and practical help in governing the kingdom; they in turn saw themselves as his natural allies, always provided that he upheld the values they most cherished by giving 'good lordship'. Thus they looked to the king for successful leadership in war, stable and just government, the advancement of existing interests and, above all, security for themselves and their family properties. Protection, indeed, was the essence of good lordship: every act of homage to the crown was conditional on it, and when protection was absent, the magnates were fully justified under feudal law in withdrawing support.

Under Henry I, relations were most troubled when England and Normandy were divided in 1100–6, and the super-magnates (those with extensive cross-Channel estates) declared for Robert Curthose in order to secure their Norman possessions. But with political union, which avoided conflicts of loyalty, Henry had little to fear, not because he terrified the magnates into submission (the traditional argument), but because most lords gained what they wanted from the king, as C. Warren Hollister (1986: 171–89) has shown. There is no question that Henry sought to weaken the magnate community by rejecting inheritance rights in principle, or by basing his regime exclusively on professional administrators; and while there was some conflict of interest between established magnates and 'new men', he kept grievances to a minimum by ensuring that both groups were included in government and enjoyed his favour. Thus, having showed how strong kingship could work *for* the magnates, Henry left behind him an aristocracy which in general believed that its interests were best served by continuing to cooperate with the crown.

On this interpretation, it follows that such tensions as existed would have been contained had the 'system' not broken down. Baronial discontent was not, therefore, the root cause of Stephen's problems, but flowed from his failure to fulfil his obligations towards the magnates as Henry I had done. Moreover, in a major article Edmund King takes the view that this was a calamity to which they responded as political realists, not as independent-minded warlords intent on exploiting the king's misfortunes. Thus, comments King, shifts in allegiance reflected 'not selfish opportunism but ... necessity' (1974: 185). Even then, few magnates were positively hostile to the crown, and no less a figure than Geoffrey de Mandeville, J.H. Round's 'great champion of anarchy', is now seen by J.O. Prestwich as 'aiming at a dominant position within the central government, not at independence of it' (1988: 299). More generally, it has also been stressed that many magnates – like their clerical counterparts – showed, through attempts to control and limit violence and disruption, a genuine concern for the stability of the realm.

Two other preliminary points must, however, be made. Generalisation about the magnates is especially dangerous, and in destroying myths about 'overmighty' subjects, it is important not to create new ones about 'undermighty' subjects. Thus David Crouch (1985) has wisely taken to task not only the view that Robert of Gloucester was a gross self-server but the counter-argument that he selflessly supported his half-sister, Empress Matilda. On the other hand, the view is still strongly held that Stephen alienated the magnates by needlessly provoking them, whereas there are good grounds for reaching a more charitable verdict. He tried to base his rule on the broad support achieved by Henry I but, as in his relations with the Church, force of circumstances compromised his political leadership at virtually every turn. As will be seen, that was due largely to the special difficulties confronting him after 1135; but a closer look at Henry I's reign warns against supposing that Stephen inherited no problems at all. Most obviously, Henry's succession plans had been supported by a powerful pro-Matilda party led by Gloucester: in consequence, Stephen inherited an already divided court, for while the Gloucester faction at first accepted the usurpation, it was never fully behind him. There were other ready-made problems, too – including a number of unresolved property claims, and the alarming fact that many magnates had English-based interests, and were thus less than fully committed to fighting for the unity of the Anglo-Norman state, even though any reverse in Normandy was bound to damage Stephen's relations with the super-magnates, his most powerful subjects. In brief, at least some of Stephen's difficulties in ensuring magnate loyalty are more readily explicable if, here as elsewhere, we remember the nature of his political inheritance.

### The growth of political discontent

The higher nobility in England numbered around fifty in 1135, and Baldwin de Redvers was the only magnate not to recognise Stephen as king. Stephen had no need to bargain for their loyalty with general promises to redress grievances as Henry I, in his coronation charter, had had to renounce William Rufus's oppressive policies. Clearly, they had not found the Henrician regime unduly exacting – only the English Church wanted reassurances that Stephen would make a fresh start. Had Gloucester remained loyal, it seems unlikely that England would have seen full-scale civil war, and his reasons for defecting to the Angevin side in 1138 have a critical significance. Yet even in 1139, with Empress Matilda in England, Stephen kept the support of most magnates, and they stood by him until 1141. Thereafter, however, few remained closely connected with the crown, and the rift was not repaired until Henry II's accession.

One obvious cause of political discontent was loss of influence at court, where the magnates were used to jockeying for favour, and resentments flourished whenever one party was advanced at another's expense. At first, a wider group benefited from Stephen's friendship than is sometimes assumed, and as few men as possible were given cause for offence. Even so, whereas Henry I had normally controlled court factions, after 1135 the crown could not so easily maintain its authority by rising above factional rivalries and dealing even-handedly with the magnates. A good example of this concerns Gloucester himself. As Henry's chief counsellor, he had played an outstanding role in public affairs, but he swiftly found himself in political limbo due to the growing ascendancy of the Beaumont twins, Robert, earl of Leicester, and Waleran, count of Meulan, who were foremost in the defence of Stephen's cause and indispensable to it; and it was probably Gloucester's resentment at his loss of position that triggered his rebellion (Crouch 1985: 231). Yet Stephen should not be blamed too harshly for this. His insecurity meant that holding the balance between court groups was always less important to him than advancing his chief allies and war captains; they, after all, had his confidence (and the strongest claims on his favour), while Gloucester was naturally distrusted because of his support for Empress Matilda before 1135. In any case, some narrowing of the court circle was probably inevitable for the additional reason that the crown's reserves of patronage had been much reduced by Henry I's grants (Green 1986: 56–61) – another limitation of Stephen's inheritance. Consequently, his ability to purchase political aid was more restricted, and once he had met the most urgent calls on his resources, little remained with which to give others a vested interest in supporting him.

But such pressures created an especially hazardous situation because of yet another major restriction on successful political management. Henry I's court had been the clear seat of power in England and (from 1106) in Normandy: there was no obvious alternative to his lordship, and he could destroy domestic enemies without too much difficulty. But as Stephen's authority fragmented under challenge from rival overlords, so disgruntled magnates could gather around them, and individual grievances might easily escalate when before they had not. Thus Gloucester's automatic response was to seek to repair his fortunes by attaching himself to the natural leader of opposition to Stephen's court, Empress Matilda. Another classic case is provided by Gloucester's ruthless son-in-law, Ranulf, earl of Chester, who nursed claims to the castle of Lincoln and the lordship of Carlisle (another legacy of Henry I's reign). When Stephen was obliged to confirm Carlisle to the Scots in 1139, Ranulf interpreted this as a sign of royal disfavour; he seized Lincoln Castle and his appeal for support from the Angevin camp led directly to Stephen's costly defeat in February 1141.

But *did* Stephen unnecessarily make a bad situation even worse? The normal view is that he was pathologically suspicious and deceitful, and that royal folly was writ large in the arrests of Geoffrey de Mandeville, earl of Essex, in 1143 and Ranulf of Chester (after a brief reconciliation) in 1146. Yet far from being irrational actions, these were emergency measures to secure the castles of especially powerful men who had supported Matilda in 1141 and were (the sources make clear) under grave suspicion of renewed treachery. Since both earls dominated their own districts, Stephen lacked the means to seize their fortresses without arresting them unawares at court, and, as has been seen (p. 20), Henry I himself had very probably made pre-emptive strikes of the same kind – without incurring criticism from modern writers, even though the pressures on him were less severe. Moreover, Stephen's initial hesitations are well attested and show his anxiety not to cause needless offence. He was astute enough to try to keep them both in his following, despite his chief advisers' objections; but ultimately he could not afford to gamble on uncertain loyalties at the expense of alienating long-term supporters who naturally expected to dominate the court. Just to underline that point, Essex and Chester, like the bishops in 1139 (p. 20), foolishly refused to give specific assurances of their good conduct, and it was only then, when their treachery seemed to be confirmed, that Stephen acted.

So the king had tried to be fair, and all he had wanted was a recognition of his authority. But by arresting subjects while under his personal protection at court, Stephen broke the normal rules and put crown–magnate relations under yet greater strain. Though they were not blameless, Essex and Chester felt they had been badly treated; they rebelled as soon as they could, and other lords kept their distance from Stephen's court because, quite simply, they did not feel safe there.

But if tension at the centre of government was one major reason for loss of confidence in Stephen's leadership, even more fundamental were his military setbacks, for these prevented him from fulfilling the first requirement of good lordship – protection of the magnates in their local power bases, their paramount concern. The critical turning-point came with the great shifts in political geography in 1141, after which Stephen could not be relied on to defend them if their estates lay outside his immediate area of control in south-east England, or to compensate them adequately if they sustained losses in his service. Geoffrey of Anjou's advances (by the end of 1141 central Normandy had fallen) were a disaster for important cross-Channel magnates like the Beaumonts, and forced them, however reluctantly, to reassess their roles. Thus Stephen was presented with a dilemma resembling the crisis of loyalty faced by Henry I when he could not hold the allegiance of the super-magnates in 1100–6. But that was far from being Stephen's only problem, since loss of effective authority in Normandy went together with divided lordship in England itself – a completely unprecedented situation. Added to this, when the Beaumonts left Stephen's service in 1141, his position in the Midlands was seriously undermined, and the overall result was that the interests of almost the entire magnate class, rather than just an influential section of it, were put at risk. Accordingly, whereas early in Henry I's reign the crown could still rely on those whose concerns were mainly English to offset disaffection among the super-magnates, from 1141 Stephen's lordship was irreversibly discredited, and it was much harder for him to maintain or regain aristocratic support.

The magnates prudently calculated the risks and adapted as best they could to safeguard their own positions. Despairing of Stephen's aid, the northern barons switched their allegiances to King David, just as others had to adjust to Empress Matilda's new supremacy in western England. Similarly, when in September 1141 Waleran of Meulan submitted to Geoffrey of Anjou in Normandy, he managed to preserve his cross-Channel estates virtually intact. Thus, other courts became more attractive than Stephen's because, by joining them, magnates gained a security that could not be theirs by continuing to fight for the crown. But, in fact, most magnates lost valuable lands whatever they did; they realised, however, that they lost least by simply withdrawing from the succession struggle and concentrating on their own survival. Thus after 1141 Stephen's closest political allies were members of the lesser nobility – the earls of Northampton, Surrey, Sussex and York being the only notable exceptions.

Where does this leave the traditional arguments about crown–magnate relations in Stephen's reign? In 1135 the magnates wished to advance their concerns by cooperating with the king, and the view that they withdrew support only when forced to do so seems to be largely justified. At both the centre and in the regions, there was the same basic reason for disquiet: namely, the crown's failure to protect them in ways they were *entitled* to expect. A more sympathetic understanding of these men (or most of them) is therefore needed, for their lack of loyalty was due more to self-preservation than to treachery or unprincipled self-interest. Yet Stephen did not impulsively create problems for the crown; rather, whereas in thirteenth-century England it was the increasingly arbitrary nature of royal rule that promoted baronial unrest, from 1135 it was the *weakness* of the crown that caused the trouble. There is, in short, little alternative but to reject the view which saw in a combination of aristocratic turbulence and royal incompetence the origin of the 'Anarchy'.

## Crisis and order

Another major theme concerns the development and exercise of magnate power in England. The corollary of a weak crown is that the magnates will flex their muscles, but not necessarily, as has so often been assumed, through natural love of lawlessness or ambition for independence. During Henry I's reign the role of the crown had become increasingly important, but after 1135 the feebler its authority became, the more vital it was for the magnates to assert their own. In particular, this reaction manifested itself in the regionalisation of magnate power, a development on which Edmund King has also thrown much light (1984). Thus, unable to rely on the crown's protection and favour, hard-headed men were thrown back on consolidating their main power bases, partly to defend themselves against rivals, partly to compensate themselves for losses elsewhere, and partly to uphold the good lordship expected of them by their own followers. Local power struggles therefore became more pronounced, as great nobles strove to assert clear-cut control over whole districts through acts of violence and land-grabbing. Yet once a magnate was established in his area, he ran it in as orderly a fashion as possible, since his reputation and authority rested on the firmness of his peace-keeping and control. There are notable examples of such regional supremacies: those of William le Gros in Yorkshire, Ranulf of Chester in the north Midlands, Robert of Leicester in the central Midlands, and Robert of Gloucester in the south-west.

Of course the magnates were not paragons of virtue; indeed, Chester's opportunism and bullying are well known. But the question remains whether their activities can be explained simply in such terms, for their strong-arm tactics were also a practical response to inadequate royal leadership, and they could work for order as well as against it. Nor were men necessarily bidding for independence of royal authority. After all, it has to be recalled that the growth of magnate power blocks was not merely a matter of private enterprise, but deliberately encouraged by Stephen and Empress Matilda alike to further their respective causes. Clear evidence of Stephen's intentions comes from his charter of c.1140 granting to Robert of Leicester the castle-borough of Hereford and lordship over the whole shire – excluding the lands of certain tenants-in-chief – with all the rights and liberties formerly enjoyed by the Conqueror's mighty earl of Hereford, William fitz Osbern. So Stephen wished to retain some direct royal influence in Herefordshire, but otherwise all its affairs were to be dealt with by Robert.

Viewed from the standpoint of Henry I's strong position, that action smacks of surrender to 'feudal anarchy'. But when writers stress such dangers, they fail to recognise that it provides a model illustration of what Stephen wanted to achieve: provincial government concentrated on one man who ruled for the crown, and who stood between anarchy on the one hand, and an overtaxed central government on the other. To be sure, magnates eagerly sought royal powers, which helped them to enforce their dominance (and keep disorder away from their own patches) in an unsettled kingdom. But that, rather than any desire for independence, was the real reason why they gobbled them up. Similarly, Matilda's earls advanced their interests on her behalf, as royal representatives controlling their shires in her name as *domina*.

The irony is, however, that whereas Stephen had to base his government firmly on the magnates, because of the influence they had gained he was all the more vulnerable to any withdrawal of their political support. Thus as loyalties wavered, so earldoms became virtually self-directing instruments of regional power. Yet while royal authority may in consequence seem to have been usurped by overmighty subjects who had deliberately set out to replace royal government with their own, that is merely an illusion created by the confused politics of the reign.

All this again suggests that the extreme accounts of baronial behaviour should be toned down. Moreover, as has been seen, when magnates parted from Stephen, the main motive was not to become independent but, once again, to defend themselves; and even if they rebelled, they did so normally as supporters of alternative overlords who, they thought, could give a more effective royal lead. But, in fact, most lords remained decidedly unwilling to challenge Stephen head on – a curious situation if they had wanted real autonomy. Evidently, it was one thing to withdraw from Stephen's court, quite another to take up arms against the crown. Rebellion thus continued to involve only a small, if powerful, section of the higher nobility, and there were only two major risings after 1141, by Essex and Chester. Then, even when Duke Henry invaded in 1153, few lords were prepared to abandon Stephen altogether. Indeed, many joined Stephen's army in a belated display of military support for the crown, and although they swiftly pressed for a settlement, it was only to secure Henry's future succession, not Stephen's overthrow. Stephen was still their lawful sovereign, and their continued reluctance to break their oaths of allegiance, despite the deficiencies of his kingship, provides a particularly striking illustration of their fundamental reverence for the crown.

Other evidence serves only to confirm the magnates' basic

respect for superior authority. Thus the coins produced in the 1140s at Leicester, Lincoln and Nottingham – towns that had passed largely out of Stephen's control – still bore the king's name. For all their local power, the earls responsible for these issues accepted the principle that they controlled the mints not in their own right but under the crown. Furthermore, when magnates issued money in their own names (very few did), George Boon (1988: 29) has suggested that this was only because they were isolated frontiersmen who could not guarantee its quality by reference to Stephen's or Matilda's authority; even then, the coins concerned normally retained a royal bust. The famous treaty between the earls of Chester and Leicester (c. 1150) was certainly no bid for baronial freedom. Each earl pledged his faith to the other, but explicitly reserved allegiance to his 'liege lord'. However independent in practice, they still could not think in terms of no feudal overlord. Ranulf of Chester had in fact given homage by 1149 to Stephen, Matilda, Henry of Anjou, and David of Scotland – remarkable testimony from a very ambitious magnate of his consciousness of higher authority – and Robert of Leicester, as co-justiciar of England from 1155 to 1168, was to play a key role in the revival of royal power after Stephen's death. The magnates, in brief, were royalists at heart.

Their conduct and conventions have provided additional grounds for questioning traditional arguments. The stability which strong regional lordship brought to certain districts is one reason for rejecting notions of endemic baronial thuggery. Another is the magnates' general reluctance to involve themselves in open revolt. Because of that, domestic politics were by no means as turbulent as they could have been; and this desire to avoid political violence is epitomised by those, including Waleran of Meulan, who joined the Second Crusade (1147–9). Rather than relishing civil war, they gained some immunity from it, the Church having taken under its protection their families and possessions. Moreover, while the code of chivalry demanded prowess and valour, it also valued prudence above fanaticism, and its precepts helped to discourage extreme forms of aggression and revenge, albeit only within the noble class. At Exeter in 1136, for example, the magnates supported Stephen's decision to show mercy to the rebel garrison, because that avoided a bloodbath and an immediate escalation of hostilities.

Again, the 'treachery' of Stephen's supporters who fled the field at Lincoln in 1141 can be interpreted as their prudently conceding defeat to stronger opponents: the day had been lost, and further violence was pointless.

What, then, of magnate feuds? It hardly needs saying that the nobles, once freed from royal control, were supposed to have increased the level of violence by engaging in protracted vendettas over land. But this was true only to a limited degree, for just as magnates often took over much of the crown's responsibility for suppressing disorder in their own areas, so they often acted to stabilise rivalries through private arbitration, marriage alliances and treaties of friendship. Indeed, busy though the royal courts had been under Henry I, magnate families could draw on considerable experience of peacefully resolving their differences without the crown's help, and their well-established mechanisms of dispute settlement were put to good use after 1135. The Chester–Leicester agreement of c. 1150 was designed to prevent violence from igniting at all, and to limit the repercussions if it did. Each earl undertook to safeguard the other's property within his district, to restrict castle-building, and to restrain his allies and vassals. These provisions, among others, suggest how two great nobles could control their respective regions with the minimum of friction, collaborate in maintaining order, and generally further mutual interests. Their agreement was the most important of the treaties sustaining what R.H.C. Davis (1990: 108–10) called 'The Magnates' Peace' of 1150–4; but such pacts were also made much earlier in the reign. Leicester, as David Crouch has shown (1986: 80–5), built over twelve years 'a national network of alliances' with his main territorial and political rivals. Chester also had understandings with the earls of Derby, Lincoln, Warwick and York; in 1149 he settled his differences with King David by renouncing his claims to Carlisle in exchange for north Lancashire. When magnates gave disputed estates to the Church – the Cistercians gained much property of this sort – that was done partly to be rid of land carrying problems with it. In such ways, rivalries were damped down, spheres of influence demarcated, private warfare checked.

The chroniclers tell a very different story, with some reason. But although baronial savagery and greed were not mere figments of their imagination, these writers – churchmen all –

had little sympathy with the magnates' predicament, exaggerated the dark side of their behaviour (especially when they failed in their duty to defend the Church), and ignored their more constructive activities. As it was, magnates and bishops often worked together for peace. At the local level, this is well seen in the cooperation between the bishop of Lincoln and the earls of Chester and Leicester (p. 71); and between the bishop of Salisbury and the earls of Cornwall, Devon and Gloucester. Nor was it as if churchmen were alone in seeking reconciliation between secular rulers. The magnates with Stephen in Normandy in 1137 recommended a truce with Geoffrey of Anjou; many northern barons would have preferred a settlement with the Scots to confronting them at the Standard in 1138; and, finally, the magnates' refusal to engage in battle at Malmesbury and Wallingford in 1153 was of critical importance for the future stability of the kingdom. In 1153 they realised that the key problem was to avoid disturbing such collective security as they had already achieved, and that the old confrontational methods of resolving succession disputes were totally discredited. Even Henry I's ousting of Robert Curthose in 1106 had been accompanied by reprisals on magnates who had backed the wrong horse, and dynastic conflict, far from ending, had continued to undermine the peace. By insisting on compromise in 1153, however, the magnates ensured that power changed hands in a strictly constitutional manner, and thus made an acceptable settlement possible for all concerned: nobility, Church and crown.

This view of the great lords as rational and responsible men cannot be pressed too far. Magnate politics were obviously more violent and much less stable in Stephen's reign than in Henry I's or Henry II's; but what differed, too, were the political circumstances. Ambitious, but anxious for their own security, magnates acted more independently because the crown's weakness left them little other choice. Their local power was awesome; but there is nothing to suggest that as a group they were chronic troublemakers or that any individual wanted to become an independent prince. Many (including even Ranulf of Chester) lost as well as gained from the disputed succession; few had any long-term interest in warfare and lawlessness. Henry II naturally insisted on major adjustments after 1154, notably gradual reduction in the number of earldoms from twenty-two to twelve and vigorous resumption of royal rights. But these adjustments were accomplished, by and large, without major protests and in a spirit of close collaboration between the magnates and the crown. A good deal of credit for this must obviously go to Henry himself; but the general willingness of the magnates to cooperate in the restoration of royal authority is still striking, and provides another, very important, reason for treating most of these men sympathetically. In sum, they had no deep-seated objections to the restoration of strong kingship because they had never really doubted its benefits. Thus King Henry did not embark on a policy of taming the magnates as a class; such a policy was simply unnecessary.

# 7
# Conclusion: the anarchy of King Stephen's reign?

The crisis of Norman power that occurred in Stephen's reign was not the product of a bungling king's mistakes, still less of self-generating anarchic forces; rather, the root causes were the *external* pressures that committed Stephen to a war of succession the like of which the Anglo-Norman state had never previously experienced. Thus the swift return to normality once the dynastic feud had finally been settled in 1153 is not as inexplicable as it sometimes appears to be.

In their panic at the gradual erosion of centralised royal government in England, and hence of the 'natural' order, contemporary chroniclers convinced themselves that chaos prevailed. Their exaggerated fears played into the hands of Angevin propagandists, and that in turn helped to create a flourishing historiographical tradition based on the notion that violence and disorder were more widespread than was actually the case. Admittedly, the extended warfare of the reign meant that suffering and disruption were experienced in England on a scale not to be seen again until the Wars of the Roses in the fifteenth century. But we must also recognise that the chroniclers, reporting only the bad news, did not acknowledge that the intensity of the hostilities varied over time and from place to place. And, above all, the view that war resulted in major disorder and lawlessness must not be distorted into the belief that it *always* did so.

Warfare went together with the dislocation of an old power structure and the creation of new ones; it thus promoted both crisis *and* order. In theory Stephen held royal authority over all England, a principle never questioned by most bishops and magnates who, given the circumstances, showed a remarkable respect for the dignity of the crown. But, in practice, by 1141 the political map resembled the position existing prior to the state-building achievements of Alfred the Great's successors – that is, the pre-tenth-century pattern of multiple provincial kingdoms. The parallel 'kingdoms' of Stephen's reign ensured that, while his own administration was confined largely to the south-east, the traditions of royal government *were* maintained elsewhere. In her western province, Empress Matilda replaced Stephen's rule with her own; even more secure and effective was King David's government of the north, where from 1141 order was maintained as firmly as could be expected in any twelfth-century realm.

Elsewhere, indeed wherever royal lordship was weak, magnate lordship came into its own, and thus another consequence of the redistribution of power was the emergence of semi-independent territories in the grips of powerful nobles. The competitiveness with which individual magnates sought regional security cannot be ignored; nor can their manipulation of local government to advance private interests. But these lords were not by nature opposed to central power; rather, the support they expected and needed was absent, and of necessity they became more assertive and self-reliant. Moreover, that response had much to do with the reinforcement of local power to *curb* instability and disorder. Thus, their alliances and control of shire government helped to create more settled conditions in an age when the state was often unable to intervene; despite superficial appearances to the contrary, the magnates were bulwarks against anarchy, especially in their own areas, where it was hardly desirable to encourage it. 'Like a king', said William of Newburgh, 'each had the power to lay down the law for his subjects' (Walsh and Kennedy 1988: 99). Once again, therefore, the disintegration of central power did not mean a total absence of effective government in the regions. Similarly, church leaders concerned themselves with promoting stability as far as they could. Both groups, rather than rejecting the concept of the crown, were in their own ways compensating for the crown's weakness; they ultimately assumed responsibility for peace-keeping nationally as well as locally; and both were thus prominent in reuniting the country and restoring the pre-1135 political order.

In sum, the period can be characterised as seeing the temporary fragmentation of England consequent on an unavoidable collapse of Norman supremacy due largely to military intervention by expansionist foreign powers. The intensification of warfare therefore had a breathtaking impact on political organisation. Short-lived though it proved to be, it halted and reversed the steady expansion of the crown's role in society and government, and thereby threw into question the state-building successes of the past two centuries. But in fact, in terms of contemporary *European* norms, the pattern that emerged was much less untypical, for England merely assumed a type of non-centralised structure conforming more or less closely to continental models. No more than in twelfth-century France or Germany did anarchy reign unchecked. An argument to the contrary would depend on the false assumption that a centralised monarchy was the only agency capable of maintaining order, and on ignoring the fact that violence and disorder, rarely ends in themselves, were often the means whereby new structures of authority and control were created. King Stephen's reign was therefore not one of genuine anarchy. It is more appropriate to think of it as a transitional period between the Norman and Angevin supremacies, when abnormal pressures meant that England experienced momentous changes in the way it was governed.

# Further reading and references

*Place of publication of books is London unless otherwise stated*

## Primary sources

Good selections of translated original sources for Stephen's reign
are given in *English Historical Documents 1042–1189*, ed. D.C.
Douglas and G.W. Greenaway, 2nd edn (Eyre Methuen, 1981),
and D. Wilkinson and J. Cantrell, *The Normans in Britain*
(Macmillan, 1987). The most important English chronicles, well
worth reading in full, are *Gesta Stephani*, ed. and trans. by K.R.
Potter, with revisions by R.H.C. Davis (Oxford: Clarendon
Press, 1976), and *The Historia Novella by William of
Malmesbury*, trans. K.R. Potter (Thomas Nelson & Sons, 1955).
*William of Newburgh, The History of English Affairs, Book I*,
ed. and trans. P.G. Walsh and M.J. Kennedy (Warminster: Aris
& Phillips, 1988), contains interesting and reliable information,
despite the fact that Newburgh did not compile his chronicle
until the 1190s. Also useful is Henry of Huntingdon's *Historia
Anglorum*, a much-needed new edition and translation of which,
prepared by D.E. Greenaway, will shortly be published by Oxford
University Press. The best source for events in Normandy (to
1141) is *The Ecclesiastical History of Orderic Vitalis*, vol. vi,
ed. M. Chibnall (Oxford: Clarendon Press, 1978).

# General surveys

R.H.C. Davis, *King Stephen 1135–1154*, 3rd edn (Longman, 1990), the standard modern analysis of the reign, is lively and very readable, though misleading in some of its conclusions. H.A. Cronne, *The Reign of Stephen 1135–54: Anarchy in England* (Weidenfeld & Nicolson, 1970), is at its best on Stephen's government. J.T. Appleby, *The Troubled Reign of King Stephen* (G. Bell & Sons, 1969), remains useful, and is rather more sympathetic to Stephen. Several textbooks offer important surveys of the reign and its background, including: F. Barlow, *The Feudal Kingdom of England 1042–1216*, 4th edn (Longman, 1988); M. Chibnall, *Anglo-Norman England 1066–1166* (Oxford: Blackwell, 1986); A.L. Poole, *From Domesday Book to Magna Carta 1087–1216*, 2nd edn (Oxford: Clarendon Press, 1955).

# Specialist works and references

Abbreviations:
ANS   *Anglo-Norman Studies*, ed. R.A. Brown (to 1989) and M. Chibnall
EHR   *English Historical Review*
TRHS *Transactions of the Royal Historical Society*

Barlow, F. *The English Church 1066–1154* (Longman, 1979).
Barrow, G.W.S. *David I of Scotland (1124–1153): The Balance of New and Old* (Reading: University of Reading, 1985).
Barrow, G.W.S. *Kingship and Unity: Scotland, 1000–1306*, 2nd edn (Edinburgh: Edinburgh University Press, 1989).
Bates, D. 'Normandy and England after 1066', *EHR*, vol. civ (1989), pp. 851–80.
Beeler, J. *Warfare in England 1066–1189* (Ithaca, New York: Cornell University Press, 1966).
Boon, G.C. *Coins of the Anarchy 1135–54* (Cardiff: National Museum of Wales, 1988).
Bradbury, J. 'Battles in England and Normandy, 1066–1154', *ANS*, vol. vi (1984), pp. 1–12.
Bradbury, J. 'The early years of the reign of Stephen, 1135–9', in *England in the Twelfth Century*, ed. D. Williams (Woodbridge: Boydell Press, 1990), pp. 17–30.

Brett, M. *The English Church under Henry I* (Oxford: Oxford University Press, 1975).

Callahan, T., Jr 'The impact of anarchy on English monasticism, 1135–1154', *Albion*, vol. 6 (1974), pp. 218–32.

Chibnall, M. (ed.) *The Ecclesiastical History of Orderic Vitalis*, vol. vi (Oxford: Clarendon Press, 1978).

Chibnall, M. 'The Empress Matilda and church reform', *TRHS*, 5th ser., vol. 38 (1988), pp. 107–30.

Chibnall, M. *The Empress Matilda: Queen Consort, Queen Mother and Lady of the English* (Oxford: Blackwell, 1991).

Cronne, H.A. *The Reign of Stephen 1135–54: Anarchy in England* (Weidenfeld & Nicolson, 1970).

Crouch, D. 'Robert, earl of Gloucester, and the daughter of Zelophehad', *Journal of Medieval History*, vol. 11 (1985), pp. 227–43.

Crouch, D. *The Beaumont Twins: The Roots and Branches of Power in the Twelfth Century* (Cambridge: Cambridge University Press, 1986).

Dalton, P. 'William earl of York and royal authority in Yorkshire in the reign of Stephen', *Haskins Society Journal*, vol. 2 (1990), pp. 155–65.

Davis, R.H.C. *King Stephen 1135–1154*, 3rd edn (Longman, 1990).

Duggan, C. 'From the Conquest to the death of John', in *The English Church and the Papacy in the Middle Ages*, ed. C.H. Lawrence (Burns & Oates, 1967), pp. 65–115.

Eales, R. 'Royal power and castles in Norman England', in *The Ideals and Practice of Medieval Knighthood*, vol. iii, ed. C. Harper-Bill and R. Harvey (Woodbridge: Boydell Press, 1990), pp. 49–78.

Edwards, E. (ed.) *Liber monasterii de Hyda* (Rolls Series, 1866).

Gillingham, J. *The Angevin Empire* (Edward Arnold, 1984).

Green, J. *The Government of England under Henry I* (Cambridge: Cambridge University Press, 1986).

Green, J. 'Anglo-Scottish relations, 1066–1174', in *England and Her Neighbours, 1066–1453: Essays in Honour of Pierre Chaplais*, ed. M. Jones and M. Vale (Hambledon Press, 1989a), pp. 53–72.

Green, J. 'Unity and disunity in the Anglo-Norman state', *Historical Research*, vol. lxii (1989b), pp. 115–34.

Green, J. 'Aristocratic loyalties on the northern frontier of

England, *c.* 1100–1174', in *England in the Twelfth Century,* ed. D. Williams (Woodbridge: Boydell Press, 1990), pp. 83–100.

Holdsworth, C. 'St Bernard and England', *ANS,* vol. viii (1986), pp. 138–53.

Holdsworth, C. 'War and peace in the twelfth century: the reign of Stephen reconsidered', in *War and Peace in the Middle Ages,* ed. B.P. McGuire (Copenhagen: C.A. Reitzels Forlag, 1987), pp. 67–93.

Hollister, C.W. *Monarchy, Magnates and Institutions in the Anglo-Norman World* (Hambledon Press, 1986).

Kealey, E.J. 'King Stephen: government and anarchy', *Albion,* vol. 6 (1974), pp. 201–17.

King, E. 'King Stephen and the Anglo-Norman aristocracy', *History,* vol. 59 (1974), pp. 180–94.

King, E. 'The anarchy of King Stephen's reign', *TRHS,* 5th ser., vol. 34 (1984), pp. 133–53.

Latimer, P. 'Grants of "totus comitatus" in twelfth-century England: their origins and meaning', *Bulletin of the Institute of Historical Research,* vol. lix (1986), pp. 137–45.

Le Patourel, J. *The Norman Empire* (Oxford: Clarendon Press, 1976).

Lynch, M. *Scotland: A New History,* 2nd edn (Pimlico, 1992).

Morey, A. and Brooke, C.N.L. *Gilbert Foliot and His Letters* (Cambridge: Cambridge University Press, 1965).

Potter, K.R. (trans.) *The Historia Novella by William of Malmesbury* (Thomas Nelson & Sons, 1955).

Potter, K.R. (ed. and trans.) with revisions by R.H.C. Davis *Gesta Stephani* (Oxford: Clarendon Press, 1976).

Prestwich, J.O. 'War and finance in the Anglo-Norman state', *TRHS,* 5th ser., vol. 4 (1954), pp. 19–43.

Prestwich, J.O. 'The military household of the Norman kings', *EHR,* vol. xcvi (1981), pp. 1–35.

Prestwich, J.O. (with comment by R.H.C. Davis) 'The treason of Geoffrey de Mandeville', *EHR,* vol. ciii (1988), pp. 283–317, and 960–8.

Russell, F.H. *The Just War in the Middle Ages* (Cambridge: Cambridge University Press, 1975).

Stenton, F.M. *The First Century of English Feudalism 1066–1166,* 2nd edn (Oxford: Clarendon Press, 1961), chapter 7.

Strickland, M. 'Securing the North: invasion and the strategy of defence in twelfth-century Anglo-Scottish warfare', *ANS*, vol. xii (1990), pp. 177–98.

Walsh, P.G. and Kennedy, M.J. (ed. and trans.) *William of Newburgh, The History of English Affairs, Book I* (Warminster: Aris & Phillips, 1988).

Warren, W.L. *Henry II* (Eyre Methuen, 1973), chapter 2.

Warren, W.L. 'The myth of Norman administrative efficiency', *TRHS*, 5th ser., vol. 34 (1984), pp. 113–32.

Warren, W.L. *The Governance of Norman and Angevin England 1086–1272* (Edward Arnold, 1987), chapter 3.

White, G.J. 'Were the Midlands "wasted" during Stephen's reign?', *Midland History*, vol. x (1985), pp. 26–46.

White, G.J. 'The end of King Stephen's reign', *History*, vol. 75 (1990), pp. 3–22.

Yoshitake, K. 'The arrest of the bishops in 1139 and its consequences', *Journal of Medieval History*, vol. 14 (1988a), pp. 97–114.

Yoshitake, K. 'The exchequer in the reign of Stephen', *EHR*, vol. ciii (1988b), pp. 950–9.